益州漢畫集

魯德福著

閻文儒

HAN TOMB ART OF WEST CHINA

A Collection of First- and Second-Century Reliefs

HAN TOMB

RICHARD C. RUDOLPH

in collaboration with

WEN YU

UNIVERSITY OF CALIFORNIA PRE

ART OF WEST CHINA

A Collection of First- and Second-Century Reliefs

ERRATA
HAN TOMB ART OF WEST CHINA

Page 5, left column: *For* southeast *read* southwest.

Page 23, left column: *Above the first line add the numeral 14.*

Page 29, No. 60: *Delete the first three sentences* (Mate . . . mate.) *and substitute:* The left half of a double-leaf tomb door. The mythical bird, probably the Red Bird of the South, differs in style from its mate, but the monster masks are essentially the same.

Page 30, No. 61: *Add the superior numeral* [1] *after claws.*
For See No. 61 *read* Mate to No. 60.

No. 62: *For* 62 *read* 63. *For* 151 *read* 160.

No. 63: *For* 63 *read* 62. *For* Mate to No. 62 *read* Mate to No. 63.

Page 42, right column: *For* 60, 61, 63, *read* 61, 60, 62, *respectively.*

NOTE.—Where there are discrepancies between measurements in inches and centimeters, measurements in inches should be considered the more accurate.

erkeley and Los Angeles   1951

University of California Press
Berkeley and Los Angeles, California

Cambridge University Press
London, England

Copyright, 1951, by
Richard C. Rudolph

Printed in the United States of America
by the University of California Press

PREFACE

WHEN THE late Paul Pelliot came to the United States after the Second World War and addressed the Chinese Art Society of America, he paid particular attention to the art of Szechwan. In speaking of the study of Chinese art in China during the war years, this internationally recognized authority on Chinese studies said:

It seems that the Chinese scholars by being forced to go to Western China [during the Sino-Japanese War] have at last felt that there was there a whole field of research which was practically untouched. All of us who have studied the ancient history of China have been struck with the fact that while Szechwan was already in Han times part of the Chinese confederation, it had a culture of its own. Han sculpture in Szechwan has quite a different character from what it has in Shantung; it is more spontaneous and more alive. . . . and I think that a survey of Szechwan ought to be undertaken.[1]

Our object has been to undertake a small part of that survey by making a study of bas-reliefs from western China. In this work are almost a hundred examples of the pictorial art of Szechwan as represented in reliefs, both in stone and clay, dating from the Later Han dynasty (A.D. 25–220). This is new material, none of it having been published in the West up to this time,[2] although a few of the reliefs have appeared in journals published in China.

We believe that these reliefs in many instances equal or surpass those of the famous Wu Liang shrine in Shantung, the publication of which greatly increased our knowledge of Han art. It is our hope that the presentation of these hitherto unpublished Szechwan reliefs will further promote the understanding of the pictorial art of first- and second-century China.

The reliefs have been reproduced by rubbings or ink squeezes, which are made by covering the relief with thin, tough, dampened paper and then tamping it down into every depression with a dry brush. When the paper has properly dried, a pad dampened with Chinese ink is applied to it, thus reproducing in black everything that projects above the background. This method, used by the Chinese for centuries, gives a full-scale facsimile of the original relief and can be applied to small or large objects, to bas-relief or sculpture in the round.

In selecting these examples of Han dynasty art we have limited ourselves in both area and type. All the reliefs, with only one exception, were found within the present borders of Szechwan Province. They are all examples of funerary art but are of two definite types. The first group comprises reliefs carved on the walls of tombs cut into sandstone cliffs or on large stone cases found within these tombs. The second group consists of scenes taken from baked pottery bricks and tiles that were used in tomb construction. The stone reliefs are classified

[1] *Archives of the Chinese Art Society of America*, vol. 1 (1945–1946), 23.

[2] After going to press, several of these reliefs have appeared in R. C. Rudolph, "Han Tomb Reliefs from Szechwan," *Archives of the Chinese Art Society of America*, vol. 4 (1950).

according to geographical origin, and a further grouping by subject matter has been attempted. This has, of necessity, been arbitrary, and unavoidable overlapping has occurred, such as the classification of mythological animals under the animal group.

Throughout this work the widely accepted Wade-Giles system of representing Chinese sounds has been used. Because it is impractical to run Chinese characters in the text, a glossary of Chinese expressions has been prepared and placed at the end of the work. Measurements are those of the maximum height and width of the object or group. Occasionally three dimensional measurements of bricks are given. We must offer a word of apology to Sinologists for frequently explaining what to them is quite obvious. An attempt has been made, perhaps not too wisely, to make this book useful to those in other fields of art, and even to the general reader as well as to the specialist. For this reason material of a technical nature is separated from the text, and certain things, long taken for granted by the specialist, are explained in some detail.

The compilation of this material would have been impossible without help received from many sources. In the first place, it would not have been started had the Western collaborator not had the opportunity to spend a year in China and study many of the reliefs *in situ* by his appointment as a Fulbright Research Scholar for 1948–1949 by the Board of Foreign Scholarships acting under the Department of State. Second, a research fund granted by the Committee on Research of the University of California, Los Angeles, provided for travel and clerical help necessary to bring this work to a conclusion. From my first days in Szechwan I was shown rubbings of various Han reliefs collected from that region by Professor Wen Yu, the learned editor of *Studia Serica*. He encouraged me to form a collection of my own, and it was through the combination of these two collections that the present work came into being. I am also indebted to Dr. Feng Han-yi, Curator of the Szechwan Provincial Museum. He was good enough to give me a rare set of rubbings of reliefs that are in the Szechwan Provincial Museum. The directors of the West China Union University Museum of Archaeology, Chengtu, were also kind enough to supply rubbings of their Han materials and to grant permission for publication.

I am profoundly indebted to the venerable Yang Chih-kao, physician and archaeologist, at whose residence in Chiating I spent many hours discussing and studying the reliefs and rubbings in his collection. Dr. Yang, although in ill health, spent much time showing me many reliefs in caves well off the beaten track which otherwise I would not have seen. His encouragement and contagious enthusiasm have proved strong stimuli. Dr. Wolfgang Franke of Peking, who has also studied the Chiating reliefs, has graciously given permission to reproduce plans of Cave I in Figure A.[a] The specific location of many of the Chiating reliefs is keyed to Franke's sketch of the vestibules appearing in Figure B. Mr. Richard Edwards, a Fulbright grantee studying in Chengtu, has rendered valuable service by providing photographs of some of the originals.

Mr. Laurence Sickman, Curator of Far Eastern Art at the William Rockhill Nelson Gallery of Art, has been kind enough to read parts of the manuscript and to make many valuable suggestions. Professor Ch'en Shou-yi of the Graduate School of Claremont Colleges has helped in many ways by generously giving of his time and knowledge. Mr. Ensho Ashikaga, my colleague in the Department of Oriental Languages, has contributed the excellent calligraphy in the glossary and bibliography. Dr. Boyd Walker of the University of California, Los Angeles, has helped by examining rubbings of fishes and suggesting tentative identifications. The maps of East Asia and the Chengtu-Chiating area are the work of my wife. I cannot close this incomplete record of acknowledgments without expressing my gratitude to the officers and faculty of West China Union University for their hospitality and coöperation. To John H. Jennings and John B. Goetz of the University of California Press go my

[a] Wolfgang Franke, "Die Han-Zeitlichen Felsengraeber bei Chiating," *Studia Serica*, vol. 7 (1948), 19–39.

vi

warmest thanks for overcoming the many difficulties that arose during the editing and production of this book.

When the unfavorable military situation caused me to leave China some months ago, Professor Wen and I planned to complete by correspondence the work that was then partly in rough draft. Subsequent developments in China have prevented our plan from being entirely successful because of the interruption of communications and the consequent loss of letters. Fortunately some additional material was received from Professor Wen before the recent occupation of Chengtu caused an indefinite suspension of our correspondence. I have therefore found it necessary to complete and revise the descriptions and to write the introduction without the much needed help of my esteemed friend and collaborator. This lamentable fact has undoubtedly resulted in errors and omissions that in no way should be ascribed to Professor Wen.

RICHARD C. RUDOLPH

University of California, Los Angeles
January, 1950

CONTENTS

PART I — Text

Introduction   3

Illustrations in Text
1. Relief of horse and rider at Chiating   9
2. Single entrance to Cave IV, Chiating   9
3. Double entrance to Cave V, Chiating   9
4. Pair of stone doors from Hsinchin   10
5. Pair of stone doors from Hsinchin   10
6. Stone door with portrait, Hsinchin   10
7. Companion scene to Figure 6   11
8. Pottery tile with hunting scene   12
9. Pottery tile with memorial pillar   12
Map of the Hsinchin-Chiating area   13
A. Scale plan of Cave I, Chiating   14
B. Plans of tomb vestibules, Chiating   15
C. Types of Hsinchin tombs   16

Descriptions of the Reliefs   21

Reliefs on Stone

   I. Chiating   21
  II. Hsinchin   26
 III. Chengtu and Lu Shan   30

Reliefs on Brick and Tile

  IV. Szechwan Province   32

Notes   39

Glossary   45

Bibliography   49

Index   65

PART II — Plates

Reliefs on Stone
   I. Chiating   1–36
    People   1
    Animals   17
    Architecture   25
    Mythology and Miscellaneous   28

  II. Hsinchin   37–67
    People   37
    Animals   46
    Architecture   50
    Mythology and Miscellaneous   54
    Tomb Doors   60

 III. Chengtu and Lu Shan   68–75
    Tomb Doors   68
    Sarcophagus   72

Reliefs on Brick and Tile

  IV. Szechwan Province   76–100
    People   76
    Animals   82
    Architecture   86
    Mythology and Miscellaneous   91

PART I

Text

INTRODUCTION

SYSTEMATIC study of Classical and Near Eastern archaeology has been in progress for about two centuries, but the study of Chinese archaeology by Western scholars began only about two generations ago. In fact, the study of China's ancient monuments may be said to have begun in Europe sometime after 1881. In that year Stephen Bushell, a British civil servant, created a stir in art circles by showing to the Oriental Congress in Berlin rubbings of some second-century bas-reliefs from northeast China. These reliefs gave the West its first idea of early Chinese painting, and were frequently referred to as paintings on stone. The reliefs were on the inner surfaces of slabs used to construct offering shrines at the Wu family cemetery near the present town of Chiahsiang in southwestern Shantung Province. These and other Shantung reliefs have been published in full, first by Edouard Chavannes, the French Sinologue, and more recently by Sekino, the Japanese archaeologist.[1]

As early as the Sung dynasty (960–1280) several Chinese archaeologists had made studies of some of the slabs, especially those bearing inscriptions. However, it was not until 1786 that Huang Yi excavated a number of slabs from the Wu shrines that had collapsed and become buried centuries earlier. Others followed his example, and now some forty-five slabs from this site are known. These slabs (generally called the Wu Liang reliefs) and the Hsiao T'ang Shan and other reliefs from Shantung remained practically the only representatives of the painting of ancient China until the recent discoveries of actual Han dynasty paintings. There are abundant references in the literature of the Han period to painters, painting, and paintings.[2] A poet of the early second century described in detail the subjects and told something of the style of the paintings on the walls of a palace that originally stood not far from the Wu cemetery.[3] It is worth noting that many parallels can be seen between these paintings, as described by this early poet, and the existing Wu Liang reliefs.

The following translation of a statement made by a famous contemporary Chinese archaeologist in 1936, after the discovery of some actual Han paintings, shows the importance that he places on the reliefs in our understanding of early Chinese art.

The position occupied by the Wu Liang reliefs in art: According to the literary records the beginnings of painting in our country can be traced back to earlier than the Chou and Shang periods. But paper and silk by their nature are frail and difficult to preserve, so the genuine examples that are seen today are not earlier than the T'ang (618–907). The lasting qualities of metal and stone exceed those of paper and silk, so pictures prior to the T'ang dynasty must be sought for among engravings on the former. The decorations on the Shang (*ca.* 1766–1122 B.C.) and Chou (1122–256 B.C.) bronzes such as the monster masks, dragons, tortoises, elephants, fish, birds, man-eating animals, and hunting scenes, are all carved with consummate skill but they belong in the category of stylized designs. Although some Han dynasty mirrors

3

illustrate such legends as the Duke of the East, Queen Mother of the West, the King of Wu, and the beautiful Hsi Shih, yet the largest of them does not exceed a foot and only a few of them are to be seen. Han dynasty pictures that still can be seen are mostly carved in stone like those of the Wu Liang shrine, the Hsiao t'ang shan and Liang ch'eng shan reliefs and those of the Teng district, but the Wu Liang reliefs are the outstanding ones. The Wu Liang memorial tablet was erected in the year 151 which places the construction of the Wu Liang shrine at the same time, one thousand seven hundred and eighty-five years ago. Thus it must be honored as the prototype of the illustration of legends, and this is not to be ashamed of.

. . . if you carefully examine the reliefs of the Wu Liang offering shrine you will realize where our system of painting originated. . . . Although they and the beautiful color paintings of later times cannot be compared with each other in style, nevertheless they have a particular charm. It is comparable to reading *The Peach Blossom Spring* after reading the prose-poems on *The Two Capitals* or eating fruit after a heavy meal. . . .[4]

Great numbers of Han dynasty bronzes, certain bricks, pottery pieces such as painted earthenware jars or the *po lu shan* incense burners, and textiles found in central Asia and the Near East,[5] all contribute to our general understanding of the art of this period. Real examples of the painting of that time, however, are in the murals and painted lacquer objects found in tombs of Han date in Manchuria and Korea, and several painted bricks from Lo-yang, Honan.

In 1920, Japanese archaeologists excavated a Chinese tomb of Han date at Liaoyang in southern Manchuria. This tomb contained murals that probably would have added considerably to our knowledge of early Chinese painting but, unfortunately, they were in a poor state of preservation. Accounts of this excavation state that the murals, done in a variety of colors, showed ceremonial feasts, people, horses, chariots, and buildings. The tomb was moved to the Port Arthur Museum, and the main paintings are said now to be beyond recognition.[6] One published photograph of a detail from a larger scene indicates that the painting was of a high quality.[7] In 1925 the Japanese excavated the tomb of one Wang Hsü in the ancient Chinese military colony of Lo-lang in Korea and found remarkable

colored lacquer paintings dating from the first century A.D. One lacquer tray about twenty inches in diameter contains a painting of Hsi Wang Mu, Queen Mother of the West, with a dragon and a tiger. An inscription on the under side of the tray is of special importance to the present study. According to the inscription, the tray was made in Shu, the old name for Szechwan, in A.D. 69,[8] thus offering concrete evidence of the far-flung contacts of the Szechwan region of that period and of one type of painting then current. This particular representation of Hsi Wang Mu closely attended by, or seated upon a throne made of, a dragon and a tiger occurs frequently on Han bricks from Szechwan and occasionally on mirrors of this period. She is represented frequently on the Wu reliefs, but never in conjunction with the two animals that seem always to be associated with her in Szechwan. Other painted and dated lacquer objects with inscriptions indicating they were made in Shu were also found in this same tomb in Lo-lang.[9]

In 1931 and 1932 two excavations of importance to the history of early Chinese painting were made by Japanese archaeologists working in southern Manchuria and northern Korea. In the first region, near the town of Ying-ch'eng-tzu, a highly complicated tomb was found consisting of four separate brick chambers with an outer protecting shell over the central structure. On both the outer and inner walls of the protected central chamber there were murals (frescoes?) on areas that had been covered over with stucco in preparation for these paintings. The subjects were mostly mythological, and the painting was crudely done with little use of color. Nevertheless, these large-scale paintings give some information on the art of that period that cannot be gained from the reliefs.[10] The second excavation brought to light a wicker basket from a Han tomb in northern Korea. Panels on the basket show paintings of ninety-four individuals in colored lacquer. Although of miniature size, these pictures give evidence of the high development of Han figure painting not conveyed by the reliefs.[11]

The most important examples of early Chinese painting are on the well-known tiles in the Boston

Museum of Fine Arts. These tiles once formed the walls and tympanum of a tomb near Loyang in central China. The lines of these colored paintings of people and animals show in the use of the brush a mastery that is a result of the discipline of calligraphic training.[12]

To summarize: mural painting and painting on silk were practiced for some centuries before the execution of the Shantung reliefs, when painting on paper was also prevalent. The few remains of actual Han dynasty painting still in existence show that it was more highly developed than the reliefs indicate and that the calligraphic element was an integral part of the technique. At the same time it should be remembered that the paintings were designed for funerary use, and the lacquer objects for everyday trade; therefore they were not of the highest level.[13] Although the actual paintings have given us valuable additional information on the development of ancient Chinese painting, the Han reliefs in general—because they are closely related to painting and provide us with innumerable examples of other techniques necessary for the understanding of the development of art, such as design, composition, and perspective—still form the most valuable corpus of material for the study of pictorial representation in ancient China.

Han dynasty reliefs of comparative value exist in Szechwan Province about a thousand miles southeast of the region where the Shantung reliefs were found. This province is regarded by outsiders as a rather remote part of China, and even Chinese scholars have more or less neglected it. As Professor Paul Pelliot has said, some impetus such as the forced migration of scholars to west China was necessary to bring about a quickened interest in this unexploited area.

Recent finds of paleolithic and neolithic artifacts prove that man has lived in this region for thousands of years. The earliest known specimens of Chinese writing—the incised inscriptions on the oracle bones at the capital of the Shang kings in central China—frequently make mention of the Shu region, showing that it was in contact with China proper around the end of the fourteenth century B.C.[14] The Chinese brought their own culture into this region some 2,000 years ago when they built a walled city and established an official residence in old Shu (Szechwan) around 300 B.C. China has suffered numerous invasions from the nomadic regions lying to the west, and this walled city was undoubtedly an early attempt to check such threats. Also around 200 B.C., hydraulic engineers constructed the irrigation and river-control systems that still function and make the Szechwan basin one of the most productive areas of China. Besides the paleolithic finds already mentioned, there are also megalithic monuments in this area,[15] and tombs dating from around the time of Christ have yielded hundreds of bronze objects, pottery figurines, and thousands of decorated pottery bricks, all in the Chinese style. There are also numerous monuments still standing, some of which bear Han dynasty dates corresponding to the first and second centuries; early Chinese archaeological works contain accounts of others now lost.[16]

At this early period the Szechwan region was carrying on a flourishing trade with foreign states and distant parts of the expanding Chinese empire. Szechwan lacquer was exported to Korea almost a century before Christ, and this trade continued to flourish into the second century. At this time also Szechwan products were being sent into India through the Burma Road region and to Canton by way of the West River (Hsi Kiang) and its tributaries. Chinese textiles were taken by caravan into central Asia and eventually found their way to the Near East and Rome. Long before this time Alexander had penetrated Asia from the west as far as northern India and the Oxus, and his followers left settlements and Greek influence in their wake with which the Chinese had frequent contact.

The spread of Buddhism in China and the extension of Chinese power into central Asia, where military settlements were established as far west as Kashgar and Yarkand, as well as the coming and going of numerous embassies and foreign traders, gave China in the period of the Han dynasty a

5

cosmopolitan atmosphere. It is not unreasonable to assume that the large volume of foreign intercourse extending over several centuries eventually had some effect upon the intellectual life of the Chinese. This could easily be true of the Szechwan region because of its geographical setting.[17] Some of this foreign influence was manifested in the local art, for Szechwan sculpture, as pointed out by Pelliot, differs considerably from that of Shantung. The *ch'üeh* in Szechwan, for example, are ornate and complex whereas those of Honan and Shantung become progressively simple. The probability of foreign influence in the *ch'üeh* has been studied by Carl Bishop and others, who amass considerable evidence to support this view.[18]

The above-mentioned Szechwan reliefs are found in the hundreds—if not thousands—of artificial caves carved by man in the red sandstone cliffs of the region. The two principal areas where these caves abound are along the Min and the Chialing rivers. Although the reliefs reproduced in this volume are limited to those found along the Min river system, near the towns of Chiating and Hsinchin, it should be pointed out that there is considerable difference between the Chialing and Min caves.[19]

The local inhabitants call these caves *man tzu tung*—"caves of the barbarians"—and believe that the original inhabitants of the area made the caves for dwelling purposes. Sufficient evidence has now been accumulated to prove that this is not true and that they are cave tombs constructed for burial.[20] However, during the time of their existence—almost two thousand years—they have been used at certain periods for dwelling places by refugees and homeless people. It is easy to imagine that during such times as the mass exterminations carried out by the blood-thirsty Chang Hsien-chung (1605–1647), these caves might have been used for temporary shelters, and likewise at an earlier period when the Chinese were still contesting with the aborigines for possession of this area. It is possible that when the Chinese were temporarily driven out, the aborigines would despoil these tombs and use them as shelters.

Thus it is not surprising that we find shards of recent date intermingled with broken figurines and shards dating from the Han dynasty. Even today these caves are put to practical use by the peasants. Many of them are used for storage places and cattle pens. It is not an infrequent sight to see houses or sheds built against the openings in the cliffs in order to use this additional space. During the recent war they served as air-raid shelters.

The illustrations in Group I are from tomb-cave reliefs found near Chiating, a town at the confluence of the T'ung and Min rivers. It is eighty air miles south of Chengtu, the capital of Szechwan Province, and about ninety miles up river from the confluence of the Min and Yangtze. I visited this region in January of last year and examined almost two hundred of these caves.

A number of the cliffs containing these caves are along the present course of the Min River, and some are in valleys caused by stream erosion. Still others are in areas away from the river where sizable streams could not have existed at the time the caves were made. Some of these locations away from the river are not well known, and hence some writers have suggested that the caves were oriented toward water. However, this is not the case. Judging from the hundreds of cave entrances I have seen, some high up on mountain sides or steep cliffs and far removed from the river, I believe that the existence of a suitable sandstone cliff was the only decisive factor in choosing a site for a cave.

The Chiating caves, of which there are hundreds, vary in depth from a few to well over a hundred feet. Although there are single caves, they are usually in groups of two or three that share a common vestibule. Single cave tombs frequently have a large vestibule or loggia with a double entrance formed by leaving a central pillar of the living rock. See fig. 3 (Cave V) and fig. B. Some of the more elaborate vestibules or portal chambers have two standing pillars, thus forming three entrances to this area from which the tombs themselves open. The largest vestibule I have seen was about seventy-five feet long and fifteen feet high. The front of it was open, with no supporting pillars, and six tomb shafts led from it into the cliff. At Chiating the reliefs are found on the walls of these vestibules and over the entrances to them. It is my opinion that these vestibules served the same function as the offering shrines at the site of the Wu tombs in Shantung, which were also decorated with reliefs.[21] This opinion is supported by the fact that ch'üeh are frequently carved in high relief on the corners of the entrances to the vestibules or tomb shafts. Two of these memorial pillars were customarily erected some distance in front of the tomb of an important person. The ch'üeh in relief at the entrances thus occupy the same relative position. In some cases it also seems possible that the men and animals carved over and near the entrances may represent the stone figures placed before tombs of the wealthy to form an avenue of approach and to act as guardians. (See figs. 1–2.) Thus there are present in some vestibules three important elements of a large surface tomb: stone figures, ch'üeh (memorial pillars), and offering shrines. In addition to these three elements, another, the shen tao or "spirit way," is probably represented by the long shaft leading to the burial itself.

It is impossible to enter the caves, which are horizontal shafts sunk straight into the cliffs, without being struck by the mathematical precision with which they were made. Their axes appear to be absolutely true, and some of the shafts are so close together that the walls have been broken through in recent times. At intervals within the caves there are steps or projections of a few inches in thickness standing out around the walls. Grooves in the floor and walls in conjunction with round holes in all four surfaces can also be seen. These irregularities in the otherwise plain walls served to keep stone doors in place, the holes in floor and ceiling serving to hold the pivots on the edges of the doors. The walls of the shafts and most of the vestibule walls have not been smoothed but still clearly show the mechanically regular and parallel striae left by the workman's chisel. Sections of the walls in some vestibules have been smoothed and divided into panels, probably in preparation for the carving of reliefs. Some of these areas, as well as others in and around vestibules and cave entrances, have been utilized in more recent times by Buddhist sculptors of the Sung dynasty, who have here and there superimposed their iconography upon the reliefs made some eight centuries earlier.

Toward the end of the shaft there are alcoves on one or both sides. They have no characteristic entrances but are simply rectangular recesses off the main shaft. The larger ones measure about seven by nine feet and frequently contain stone cases which will be discussed later. Small recesses that are about two feet deep and eight feet long represent kitchens. On the end of the recess farthest from the shaft entrance there are one or two fireplaces carved from the living rock. In a few instances these fireplaces are placed at the end of the shaft. The rest of the small recess is raised somewhat above the fireplaces and served as a shelf for utensils and grave articles. The existence of these "fireplaces" has led some observers to the conclusion that the caves were designed as dwellings. Any number of arguments can be brought forth to refute this theory. For example, the caves would not be of such great depth, nor would fireplaces be placed in such a position to fill the cave with smoke. It is probable that they served the same role as the miniature pottery stoves usually found in Han tombs.

Some distance beyond this area in another side chamber are stone cases, which have been hollowed out but not detached from the wall or floor. Sometimes they are single, sometimes in pairs with a common partition. The natural tendency is to regard them as coffins, but their large size and the presence of baked pottery coffins are strong arguments against this conclusion. Perhaps they served as coffers instead of coffins and were used to preserve some of the possessions of the deceased. The shaft usually extends a few feet beyond this side chamber and then comes to an abrupt halt. A definite downward slope toward the entrance from the shaft end can sometimes be observed. This may have been to provide drainage. (See fig. A.)

7

Group II comprises reliefs found in cave tombs near Hsinchin, a small town about twenty-five miles southwest of Chengtu and sixty miles north of Chiating. The Hsinchin caves differ from those found at Chiating. The impressive vestibules found in the latter place are lacking, and the shafts of the Hsinchin tombs are quite short. The tombs here are usually rooms—either a single one or a connected series—carved out of the red sandstone and connected to the face of the cliff by a short passageway that is blocked up and concealed. The Chinese archaeologist Shang Ch'eng-tso has studied the Hsinchin tombs and classifies them according to three types: single, double, and developed.[22] (See fig. C.)

One of the outstanding and interesting characteristics of the Hsinchin tombs is the presence in many of the rooms of stone boxes fitted with lids. These boxes are carved out of a single block of red sandstone and are not attached to the wall or floor as at Chiating. They are quite large, measuring about eight feet long, three feet wide, and three to four feet high. Although they have been called coffins or sarcophagi, this terminology is open to question. Because the point is controversial and cannot be finally settled until a hitherto unplundered tomb can be scientifically excavated, they may be referred to as coffers for the present. Shang Ch'eng-tso paid particular attention to this problem in his study of the Hsinchin cliff tombs and makes three points in this connection: all caves have pottery coffins; these do not always have stone coffers; all those with stone coffers have pottery coffins. Shang acquired this information through hearsay, but he considers it reliable enough to prove that the stone boxes were not coffins. He also personally examined a number of boxes that had not been removed from the caves, and he found they contained only mud and Han dynasty coins, with absolutely no trace of bone. Furthermore, he argues that these large stone boxes did not serve as outer coffins for the baked pottery coffins, because the latter, although quite narrow, are usually too long to fit into the former. Shang comes to the conclusion that the stone boxes were used to contain the clothing and prized possessions of the deceased.[23]

These stone coffers, although difficult to remove from the caves, are eagerly sought by both peasant and scholar. Whole coffers are used by the local inhabitants for water- or feed-troughs for their cattle; if they cannot be removed from the tomb, they are broken up and the large slabs of the sides and ends are used for building or other purposes. The artist and archaeologist seek them because they are the main source of the Hsinchin reliefs. As stated above, these tombs have no vestibules to receive funerary decorations, and the walls of the shafts or chambers were not utilized for this purpose; consequently these decorations were placed on sides of the coffers. Some more or less formalized reliefs appear also on the few Hsinchin stone doors that still exist, but it is principally the coffers which provide a rich and variegated supply of Han pictorial art.[24]

It is rather surprising, since these places are only sixty miles apart and are on the same river, that the architecture of the tombs should differ so much. This quite naturally leads to differences in the subject matter of the reliefs. At Chiating the Han sculptors used rows of tile ends and other similar devices to give the vestibules the appearance of brick and tile structures—probably offering shrines. The absence of vestibules at Hsinchin eliminates such architectural decorations, but on the other hand the four surfaces of the rectangular coffer suggest other motifs.

Also surprising is the difference in the techniques employed in rendering the reliefs. The Hsinchin reliefs have a conspicuous crosshatch background (sometimes not shown in our rubbings), and in most instances the striations go right through the figures, giving them a peculiar striped effect in the rubbings (No. 37). The Chiating reliefs have either a smooth background or one of parallel striations left by the workmen who hollowed out the vestibules or surfaced the façades. Except for the intentional incised decoration the surface of the Chiating figures is smooth. One apparent exception to this general characterization is the spectacular and beautifully conceived tiger (No. 19) in Cave VIII, which is reminiscent of the Hsinchin style.

8

Fig. 1.
Relief of horse and rider
at Chiating (see No. 17).

Fig. 2.
Single entrance to Cave IV,
Chiating.

Fig. 3.
Double entrance to Cave V,
Chiating.

Fig. 4. Upper left.
Pair of stone doors
from Hsinchin (see Nos. 60–61).

Fig. 5. Lower left.
Pair of stone doors
from Hsinchin (see Nos. 62–63).

Fig. 6. Lower right.
Stone door with portrait,
Hsinchin (see No. 64).

Fig. 7.
Companion scene to figure 6
(see no. 65).

Fig. 8.

Pottery tile

with hunting scene (see No. 76).

Fig. 9.

Pottery tile

with memorial pillar (see No. 87).

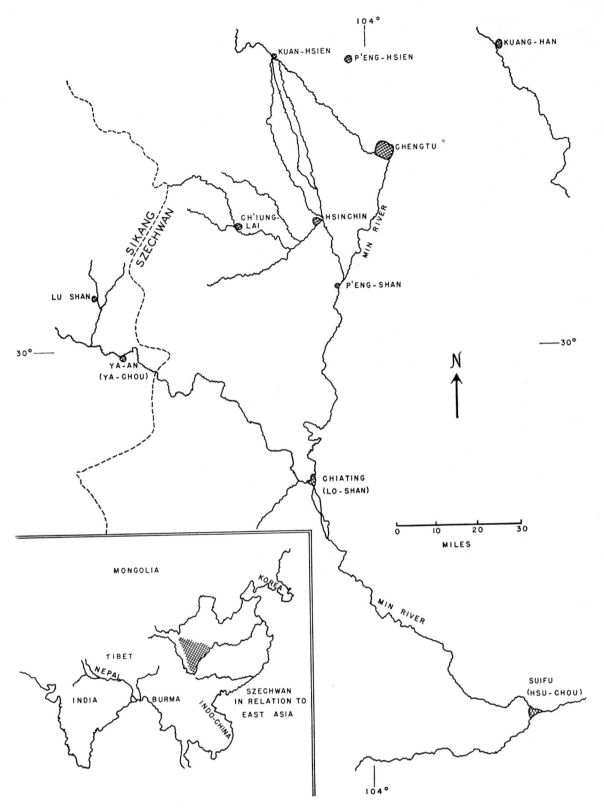

Map of the Hsinchin-Chiating area.

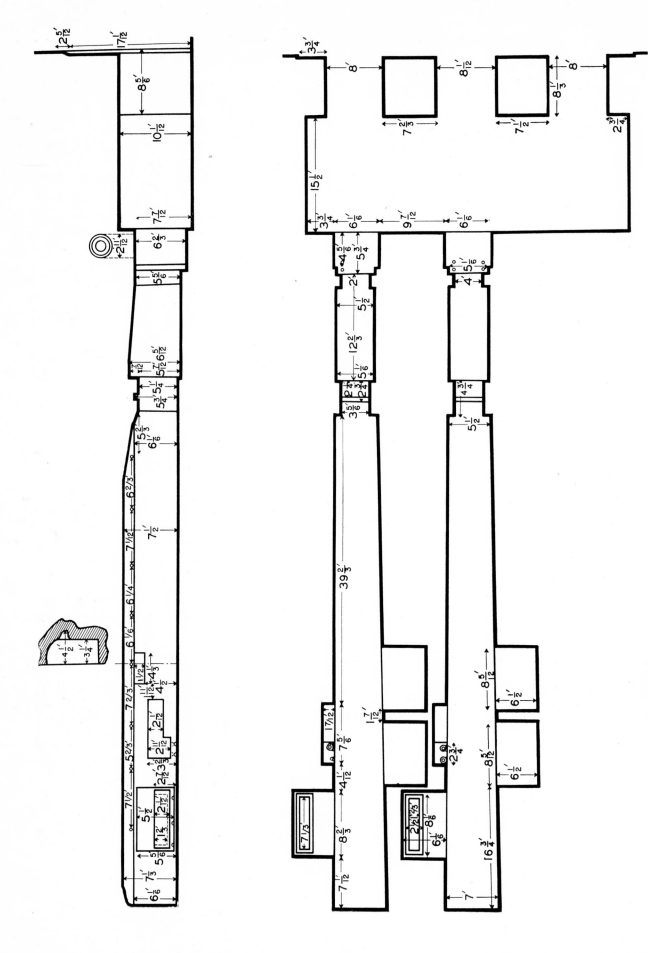

Fig. A. Scale plan of Cave I, Chiating. Scale 1/120 full size. *After a drawing by Yang Wei, 1941.*

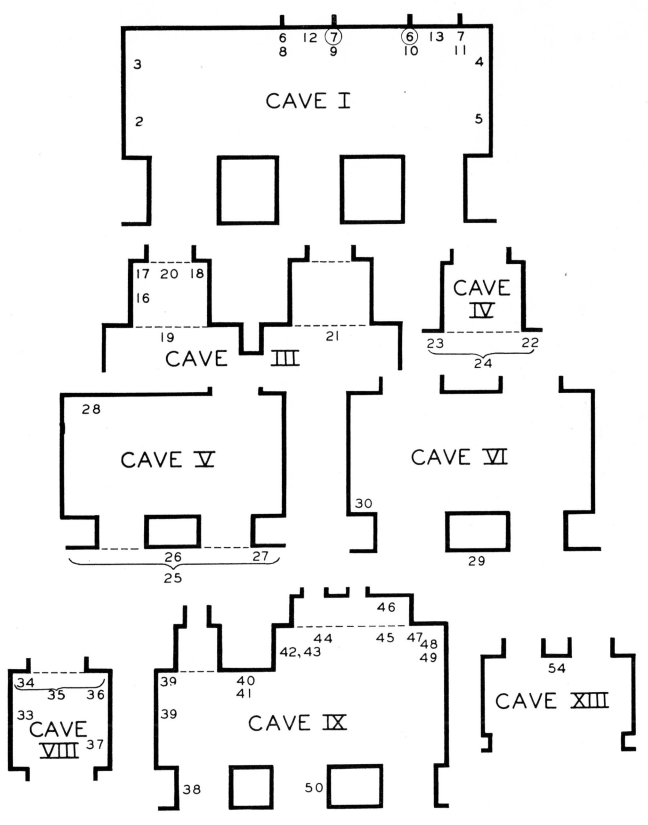

Fig. B. Plans of tomb vestibules, Chiating.

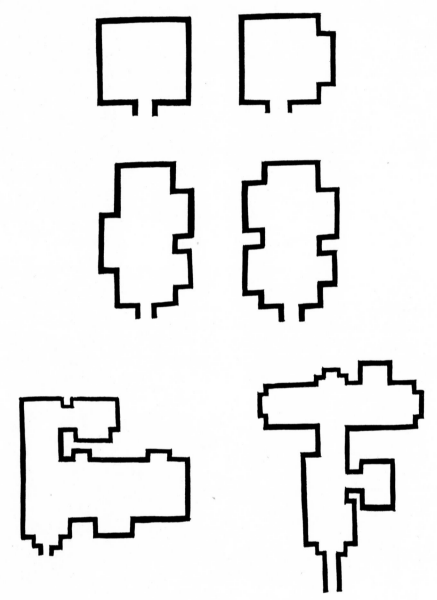

Fig. C. Types of Hsinchin tombs.

This figure, perhaps because of its position in the vestibule, is the best preserved of the Chiating reliefs with the possible exception of some architectural designs in higher relief. But it is not its condition alone that differentiates it from others in this region. Even with allowance for the difference in preservation, there still remains an obvious contrast in which the background and execution of this relief closely resemble the techniques employed at Hsinchin. Is it possible that a visiting Hsinchin artist was invited to give a practical demonstration of his skill in the Chiating vestibule?

Generally speaking, all the reliefs of these two regions, with the exception of the *ch'üeh* and some other architectural decorations, can be said to be in the low style. When considering the technical aspects of the reliefs, the structural differences between the Chiating and Hsinchin tombs and the resultant differences in the locations of the reliefs must be considered. Those at Hsinchin have been well protected from the ravages of the subtropical climate of this part of China. But those at Chiating have been either directly or indirectly exposed to the prevailing high humidity and to frequent torrential rains. The effect that this exposure has had upon the soft red sandstone of the Chiating reliefs during the past eighteen or twenty centuries is not difficult to imagine. The freshness of the protected Hsinchin reliefs as contrasted with the weather-worn figures from Chiating is apparent at first glance. It should also be remembered that rubbings, although giving a true facsimile, tend to overemphasize some aspects of the original and underemphasize others. A word of apology must be offered here about the inconsistent quality of the Chiating and Hsinchin rubbings. The main reason for this is that these rubbings are not made commercially and cannot be purchased in the open market. Some of the best Chiating reliefs are only a few hundred yards from the town, but I could not find a single rubbing in any of the shops where this type of thing is ordinarily sold. It was only with the assistance of Chinese friends that I was able to secure a set of Chiating rubbings and many from Hsinchin. They were made by several rubbing makers, and this accounts for the omission or inclusion of backgrounds and other differences.

It may be well at this point to make a few general comparisons between Szechwan reliefs, represented by the above groups, and those from Shantung. The Szechwan work is in much higher relief than the latter, but perhaps the most obvious difference is the lack of organization in many of the Szechwan scenes. Reliefs are frequently scattered about the walls of a large vestibule with little or no relation to each other. But the scenes in the Wu reliefs are well integrated, carefully planned, and conceived on a grand scale. Much of this difference may be due to the fact that the Shantung shrines were planned and erected at a specific time for certain people whereas this was not always the case in Szechwan. There is reason to believe that some of the Chiating vestibules originally were made larger than necessary with an eye to future use; and sometimes a small vestibule was enlarged at a later date to accommodate more shaft openings. In many of the vestibules the walls have been smoothed and divided into rectangles for future reliefs which did not materialize. The open background and undecorated space between figures make it obvious that the principle of *horror vacui* did not have the popularity with the Szechwan artists that it had with those in Shantung. Moreover, the Szechwan figures are not so stylized as their northeastern contemporaries, nor are they placed in such formalized settings. Finally, most Szechwan scenes representing action have a more dynamic quality than parallel scenes in Shantung. These last three aspects of the Szechwan reliefs seem to substantiate Pelliot's contention that "Han sculpture in Szechwan has quite a different character from what it has in Shantung; it is more spontaneous and more alive. . . ."

Large quantities of grave goods have been gathered from the tombs of the Chiating and Hsinchin regions. The West China Union University Museum of Archaeology possesses more than a thousand of these objects. Bronze basins, mirrors, lamps, weapons, and crossbow mechanisms have been found in limited number, and quantities of early and late Han coins have come to light. A few iron swords have been recovered, and Shang Ch'eng-tso claims to have seen a silver bowl that came from one of the cliff tombs. All the usual Han pottery objects are also represented among the grave goods and have been found in quantity. There are figurines of servants, officials, soldiers, musicians, dancers, real and mythical animals, utensils, ritual vessels, and models of houses, stoves, well-curbs, and other objects.[25]

In group III there are eight rubbings of stone reliefs, four of them from tomb doors found near Chengtu and four from the sides of a dated sarcophagus found at Lu Shan. This place is just over the border in Sikang. One of the reliefs (No. 75) from this actual stone coffin (to differentiate it from the Hsinchin boxes) provides a unique contribution to Han archaeology.

Group IV of the illustrations reproduces rubbings of bricks used in tomb construction and some that have been found in sandstone burial caves. From the thousands of tomb bricks found in this region it may be assumed that their manufacture was the result of a thriving industry. So numerous are Han dynasty brick tombs in this region that it is not at all uncommon to see whole bricks or fragments of them in recently constructed walls. In a like manner, beautiful glazed tiles, ridge ornaments, and finials from the Ming palaces are being dug up at Nanking and sold to cement factories.

There are so much freedom and artistic quality in the composition and execution of the scenes on some of the large bricks, among which there are few duplicates, that at first glance we are likely not to think of them as being products of a mold. But the smaller ones, judging from the large number found that are absolutely the same in both geometrical and pictorial designs, obviously were mass produced by the mold method. It is possible that these small ornamented bricks were stamped with wooden dies that had the design carved in intaglio (No. 100), but it is more probable that they were made in releasable or "draw" molds that permit the drawing away, without injury to the soft clay, of the part of the mold that bears the design.

Baked pottery bricks and tiles have been used in other parts of China for the construction of tombs of the same general period or even earlier. The most impressive of these come from modern Honan Province, some six or seven hundred miles northeast of Szechwan. These are large hollow tiles measuring almost six feet in length and two feet in breadth. The formalized decoration of these tiles was accomplished by pressing dies into the slab of clay before baking, leaving the design in intaglio rather than in relief.[26] In many instances the workman was careless in his use of the die, and impressions of its edge can be seen in the finished tile. Some sixty of these spectacular tiles are in the Royal Ontario Museum in Toronto and have been the subject of a special study.[27] Smaller Han dynasty tiles were used here as well as in other parts of China, but the larger Szechwan tiles are a group apart and provide new material of great artistic value.

In his study on the hollow tomb tiles of the Han dynasty, Wang Chen-to divides Han bricks and tiles into five general classes:

1. Narrow rectangular bricks (*t'iao*) used in walls of various kinds and in tomb construction. These are frequently used as headers and binders. The following works contain collections of this type of brick: *Ch'ien p'i t'ing chuan lu, T'un an ku chuan ts'un, Mu t'ao hsüan ku chuan t'u lu.*

2. Square tiles, to cover surfaces. The *Kuang ts'ang chuan lu* contains examples of this type.

3. Inscribed bricks. Some are used to record burials, such as those of the Han criminals, whose fragmentary epitaphs are collected in the *Heng nung chung mu yi wen.* Some of them were used to record personal affairs, such as the bricks showing deeds to land in the *Chuan men ming chia.*

4. Miscellaneous bricks used as supports of various kinds and bases for pillars.

5. Tomb tiles (*k'uang chuan, k'ung chuan*). They vary in shape and size and differ from the other classes in that they are hollow and both ends have holes in them. For this reason they are currently called hollow tiles (*k'ung chuan*). They are also called lute tiles (*ch'in chuan*), because of the sound they emit when used as a sounding

board, and district guardian tiles (*t'ing chang chuan*), from the picture of this official which occurs on many of them. These large hollow tiles are used for building tombs and other structures.[28]

Hollow tiles have not been found in Szechwan, but the other four classes occur there. The first class is especially common (Nos. 84, 88, 89, 96, 97, 98) but, being mass produced, does not have the artistic quality of the second class, which, in Szechwan at least, is much less common (Nos. 76, 77, 78, 79, 80, etc.). We have included examples of the third class (inscribed bricks) only when they occur in conjunction with pictorial material, because the latter is our prime interest. For the same reason no examples of the fourth class are included.

Inscriptions, as pointed out above, occur on Han dynasty bricks, and large numbers of them have been found in Szechwan. The content of the inscriptions varies and includes dates expressed by both cyclical characters and *nien hao*, name of the maker, name of the person in whose tomb they were used, and felicitous wishes.

Of greater importance are datable inscriptions that occur in the cliff tombs. Five have been found near Chungking, and several in the Chiating region.[29] Hung Kua, writing in the twelfth century, records a seventy-four-character inscription, dated A.D. 77, from a Han cliff tomb in Szechwan the location of which is no longer known.[30] Wolfgang Franke plans to make a special study of these inscriptions, so they will not be discussed here. Several bear dates corresponding to the first century, but the majority are second-century inscriptions.

Apart from their artistic value, the Szechwan reliefs, in common with other early pictorial materials, are of value for the insight they give into the daily life, material culture, folklore, and beliefs of the people who created them.[31]

We have, among others, illustrations of games and feasts (Nos. 11, 12, 56, 57, 77, 78, 79, 80), hunting (Nos. 76, 91, 92), fishing (Nos. 11, 12), and harvest (No. 76). Excellent architectural details are shown (Nos. 25, 26, 27, 50, 51, 86, 87, 90), and we are given at least some idea of commerce (No. 93), and industry (Nos. 91, 92). A large number of horses are shown (Nos. 17, 18, 39, 46, 85, etc.), and transportation is represented by various types of vehicles drawn by both man and beast (Nos. 5, 52, 53, 82, 83, 84, 90). Most representations of people give information on the costume of that period (Nos. 37, 64, 65, 68, 77, 78, 79, 80, etc.), and many of them show military equipment (Nos. 6, 37, 43, 51, 68, 70, 85).

One historical scene, the attempted assassination of Ch'in Shih Huang Ti in the third century B.C., occurs twice in the Chiating reliefs (Nos. 13–14, 15–16). This event is depicted three times in the reliefs of the Wu offering shrine in Shantung, and one of them resembles one of the Chiating scenes so closely (see No. 16) that the one may have served, directly or indirectly, as a pattern for the other, or both may have had a common origin.[32] Two favorite subjects in the Shantung reliefs— Ch'in Shih Huang Ti vainly trying to recover a sacrificial tripod from the river (Chavannes, Nos. 52, 122, 148, 1266) and the infant King Ch'eng with his loyal counselor the Duke of Chou (Chavannes, 48, 73, 128, 147, 1224, 1262)—have not been found in the Szechwan reliefs.

Mythological scenes are many. Hsi Wang Mu, the Queen Mother of the West, sits on her tiger-and-dragon throne and receives homage from weird beings and fabulous animals (Nos. 96, 97, 100), sun and moon symbols are transported and held aloft by fantastic creatures (Nos. 58, 59, 94, 99), and symbolical or ferocious animals indicate directions or guard the sleep of the dead (Nos. 24, 47, 49, 72, 73, 74, and 19, 20, 71).

We confess our inability to explain certain designs and scenes, and hope that other workers will throw light on these things for us. We make no attempt at artistic interpretation, although some scenes on the large bricks (Nos. 77–80, 85, 86, 91, 92), portraits (Nos. 44, 45, 64, 65), animals (Nos. 17, 18, 19), and some of the more complex compositions (Nos. 28, 29, 54, 55, 56, 76) may offer material of interest to the art expert as well as to laymen.

DESCRIPTIONS OF THE RELIEFS

Reliefs on stone

I. Chiating

1.   Size: 18 × 73½ in. (45.5 × 188 cm.)
Location: Cave I (2)
A group of four adults and three (?) children. The person on the right seems to be admonishing a kneeling adult. A gesticulating child is pleading or dancing with the central adult figure. To the left of the latter is a person sitting on the ground. From its size it seems to be larger than the two children but smaller than the adults; the present condition of the stone suggests a dwarf. On the far left a child is receiving some object from an adult.

2.   Size: 19½ × 72 in. (51 × 188 cm.)
Location: Cave I (3)
Procession of seven people. The one on the left is drawing a cart that seems to have solid wheels and a figure riding inside. The other people are following the cart. One is leaning on a staff, and another is carrying something on a pole over one shoulder.[1] See No. 5.

3.   Size: 24¾ × 50½ in. (63 × 127.5 cm.)
Location: Chiating
A person leaning on a stick, and two kneeling figures in attendance. This has a strong resemblance to the two scenes of the filial Po Yu (Po Yü) in the Wu reliefs.[1] His mother frequently beat him with a stick, and in his youth her blows hurt but he was glad that she was strong; in later life he cried because her blows had become feeble.

4.   Size: 24 × 47 in. (61 × 119.5 cm.)
Location: Cave IX (40)
A divinity or an important personage surrounded by people who seem to be worshipping or paying homage, except for the large figure on the left. The smaller figures are reminiscent of the donors in the numerous Hsi Wang Mu scenes in both the Szechwan and Shantung reliefs. See Nos. 96, 97, 100.

5.   Size: 22½ × 39½ in. (57 × 100 cm.)
Location: Cave IX (49)
A man pulling a small covered cart with a figure inside. Two people appear to be following. See No. 2.

6.   Size: 38 × 43 in. (95.5 × 109.5 cm.)
Location: Cave V (26)
Stylized figure of a man testing or cocking a crossbow. The bow itself is held on the ground by his feet while he pulls on the bowstring with both hands. The great arms and legs, lack of a trunk, and the high headdress give him a striking appearance. A similar design, die-stamped, occurs on a Han tomb brick from Honan.[1]

7. Size: 28½ × 54 in. (71 × 138 cm.)
Location: Cave I (6)
A large human figure, apparently a guardian. In his right hand he holds something like a club. On his head he wears something that appears to be an animal mask. In this respect this and the following figure bear some resemblance to a horned guardian relief found in a Liao tomb in southern Manchuria.[1]

8. Size: 18½ × 39 in. (47 × 99 cm.)
Location: Cave III (17)
A large human figure that appears to be wearing an animal mask with horns. He is holding objects resembling a weapon and a snake in his right and left hands respectively. The relief is not clear enough to determine precisely what type of ornament is upon his head. Although there are many differences, this relief recalls the Shantung relief showing one man holding a snake being attacked by a second man with a weapon similar to the one shown here.[1] A further parallel is found in a fresco from a Han tomb in Ying-Ch'eng-tzu. This scene shows a guardian wearing a spiked crown and holding a banner and snake in his right and left hands respectively.[2] A similar type of guardian occurs several times in the Chiating caves.

9. Size: 22½ × 48½ in. (56 × 124.5 cm.)
Location: Cave I (7)
A large human figure, probably a servant. In his right hand he holds a stafflike object (broom?) and in his left what appears to be a basket. Clay figurines quite similar to this—servants holding brooms and dust baskets—have been found in Han tombs near Chengtu and can be seen in the West China Union University Museum.[1] Since this particular type of servant is found in Szechwan in both stone and clay but not in published collections from other regions, it may be peculiar to ancient Shu.[2]

10. Size: 19 × 37 in. (48.5 × 93.5 cm.)
Location: Cave III (18)
A human figure wearing what appears to be a feline mask. In his right hand he is holding an object resembling a shepherd's crook.

11. Size: 12½ × 15½ in. (31 × 39 cm.)
Location: Cave IX (47)
A kneeling fisherman. He has bare legs and a strange headdress; indistinct as this relief is, the figure gives the impression of being a "barbarian," that is, a non-Chinese. This scene is in a corner of the cave with the fishing pole directed toward the adjoining wall on the right. See No. 12.

12. Size: 6 × 15 in. (15 × 38 cm.)
Location: Cave IX (48)
A cyprinoid fish. Its ventral mouth and long dorsal fins suggest the possibility of its being a *Labeo*. It is in the same corner as No. 11 but on the wall that joins the one bearing the fisherman. This fish is probably the one the man is angling for, although it is not in the position we expect since its tail points toward the man.

13. Size: 11½ × 117½ in. (29 × 300 cm.)
Location: Cave III (19)
The attempted assassination of Ch'in Shih Huang Ti in 227 B.C. This event is depicted three times in the Wu reliefs.[1] The present scene differs from the traditional ones by the absence of the box containing the head of the king's enemy Fan Yü-ch'i, by presentation of which the would-be assassin Ching K'o gained access to the king's presence. The kneeling figure of Ch'in Wu-yang, Ching K'o's conspirator, seen in the traditional scenes, is absent here. To the right, Ching K'o is struggling with a person who has seized him. This figure probably represents the king's doctor Hsia Wu-chü. The scene shows the King of Ch'in fleeing—to the left. Between the two is a pillar resembling the *erh chu* (cf. No. 35). This event is described in detail in Ching K'o's biography in Ssu-ma Ch'ien's *Shih chi* of the first century B.C.[2] Of the three assassination scenes in the Wu reliefs, this scene resembles Chavannes No. 75 (Sekino No. 53) more closely than the other two. Perhaps the most conspicuous difference between this Chiating relief and the Shantung reliefs is the absence of the dagger thrown by Ching K'o, which was supposed to have penetrated a bronze pillar. As Bodde showed, this is a later embellishment.

This is the left section of a long frieze and a continuation of No. 13. The four figures in this section of the relief are unclear because of its being in an exposed place, where it suffered from the elements. The figure on the right appears to be a grotesque figure brandishing a weapon. The next is that of a man with a tall headdress who is gesturing toward some indeterminate object. On the far left is a person, evidently of high station, who is observing the scene from a dais. This undoubtedly represents the same scene as Nos. 40 and 41 and has no connection with the assassination scene.

15. Size: 25 × 166 in. (63.5 × 418.5 cm.)
Location: Cave IX (39)
The attempted assassination of the King of Ch'in. The two figures in the center are those of Ching K'o, the would-be assassin, and a man who has seized him, probably the king's doctor. In front of them is the king fleeing for his life, and in front of him two other running people. Between Ching K'o and the king is a pillar. In the Wu Liang scene of this same event Ching K'o, after being seized, hurled his sword at the king in a last desperate attempt on his life, but it lodged in the pillar between the two. This part of the picture is based on a later exaggeration of the *Shih chi* account. In the present scene there are two indeterminate objects near the pillar which at first glance somewhat resemble a serpent coiled around the pillar. But the upper object must certainly be Ching K'o's sword, and the lower one the king's sleeve, which was torn off in the struggle according to the *Shih chi* account. And indeed the king's arm nearest to the pillar is obviously bare. In one of the Wu reliefs sleeve and sword are in the same positions as here, in another the sleeve is on the other side of the pillar, and in the third it is still on the king's garment.[1] See No. 16 for the continuation of this scene.

16.
Behind Ching K'o and the soldier is Ch'in Wu-yang kneeling near the head of Fan Yü-ch'i. At the extreme right is a soldier that may be part of another composition. The Szechwan and Shantung assassination scenes resemble each other so closely they must have had a common origin. (See note 32.)

17. Size: 42¼ × 54 in. (107.5 × 137 cm.)
Location: Cave I (1)
Large horse with rider. The horse has a knotted or decorated tail and head ornament. The rider is holding some object, perhaps a weapon. In general the horses on the Han reliefs of Szechwan are very much like those on the Shantung reliefs and resemble the Bactrian horse brought in from the West.[1] (See fig. 1.)

18. Size: 19½ × 54½ in. (49 × 138 cm.)
Location: Cave IX (42)
A man trying to control a horse by means of a rope. The horse shows great animation and seems to be shying at or attacking some unrecognizable object in front of it. A similar motif was used on the large Honan tomb tiles.[1]

19. Size: 36 × 53 in. (91.5 × 134 cm.)
Location: Cave VIII (33)
A leaping tiger. His contorted appearance is very similar to those on Han reliefs found in Nan-yang, Honan, the main difference being that in the Nan-yang examples the head is shown in profile and here it is front face. This magnificent beast has rudimentary wings similar to those on the Lu-Shan tiger (No. 72). The vestibule in which this scene occurs has been named Tiger Cave (*lao hu tung*).

20. Size: 24½ × 24½ in. (62 × 62 cm.)
Location: Cave VIII (34)
A mastiff with harness attached to a rope. Pottery dogs of the same appearance and with the same type of harness have been found in Han dynasty tombs in Szechwan. One such figurine that could have served as a model for this relief is now in the West China Union University Museum.[1]

21. Size: 7 × 18¾ in. (18 × 48.5 cm.)
Location: Cave V (27)
Probably a shark. In China and India they are found in the higher reaches of the larger rivers.

22.   Size: 9 × 16½ in. (23 × 41.5 cm.)
Location: Cave V (28)
A cyprinoid or carp. The fins and body form suggest *Carassius auratus*.

23.   Size: 21½ × 25 in. (54 × 64 cm.)
Location: Cave IV (23)
A reclining ram or sheep. (See fig. 2.)[1]

24.   Size: 11 × 17½ in. (28 × 44.5 cm.)
Location: Cave IX (41)
The Red Bird, symbol of the South, according to ancient Chinese cosmology.

25.   Size: 18½ × 41½ in. (47 × 106 cm.)
Location: Cave III (16)
Two people, the one on the right kneeling, before a house or shelter with tiled roof. The person on the left appears to be holding out an object resembling the so-called symbol of authority. The interior of the house is not very clear, but the remains of what is probably a seated figure can be seen. This relief is included because of its resemblance to one of the filial-piety scenes in the Wu reliefs. The original stone no longer shows the scene clearly, but a drawing of it published in 1821 resembles the Chiating scene very closely.[1] In this early drawing after the original, there is a son bowing to "the image of Hsiu-ch'u" under a shelter similar to the one in our rubbing while a figure in the background looks on. This image is probably that of the wife of Hsiu-ch'u, who once held sway in what is now Kansu

26.   Size. 24 × 38 in. (60 × 95 cm.)
Location: Cave IX (46)
A house and man. The figure on the left is carrying something on a staff across his right shoulder. With his left hand he appears to be holding a rope that is attached to two unrecognizable objects. Although much of this relief is indistinct, it shows the roof construction rather clearly.[1]

27.   Size: 25¼ × 43 in. (65 × 109.5 cm.)
Location: Cave XIII (54)
A badly damaged *ch'üeh* that shows very interest-

ing details of construction and decoration. Representations of these structures occur frequently at the entrances of the vestibules or the caves proper. This fact may be adduced in support of the argument, if any still be needed, that these caves were designed for burial of the dead and not for shelter of the living. Surface tombs of the same period in this area as well as others were frequently marked by the actual *ch'üeh*. Hence the pseudo *ch'üeh* in relief at the entrances to caves gave mute warning to the visitor that he was approaching a tomb. These *ch'üeh*, especially those which cover both faces of the corner formed by an entrance, provide the highest relief sculpture that was found in any of the caves.

28.   Size: 27 × 177 in. (68 × 455 cm.)
Location: Cave VIII (35)
A large tiger, symbol of the West, above a bow-shaped support known as the *erh chu*. (See No. 35.) Under the tiger's forequarter is a kneeling archer about to shoot at a bird under the tiger's belly. Behind the tiger is the head of a snake whose body is coiled around the right part of the bow-shaped support. Directly below the support is the coin pattern called *ku ch'üan wen* so frequently seen in Han tomb decorations.[1]

29.
The left part of No. 28. A long dragon, symbol of the East, opposes the tiger. Below its tail is a figure resembling a child standing on its head; under its belly is a toad, frequently used as a symbol for the moon. Between the dragon and the tiger is an unclear object that may be a tortoise and snake, symbol of the North.

Standing on the head as a sport is referred to in Han literature and represented in Han art. Although this may have no more significance than the apparent acrobatic scenes in the Wu Liang reliefs, it is possible that this attitude has some special meaning when it appears in tombs. Besides this Szechwan example, a fresco in a Han dynasty tomb in Liao-yang in southern Manchuria shows a man preparing to stand on his head.[1]

30–31.   Size: 28½ × 137 in. (72.5 × 348 cm.)
Location: Cave IV (24)
Tile ends, humans, and animals. Directly under the tiles on the far right and left are two unidentifiable objects, and between them are four rectangles representing beam ends. Under the third tile from the left, two birds are examining or eating something. Six seated figures occupy the center of the relief, apparently observing the scene below. This consists of a graceful, long-sleeved dancer flanked by two weird-looking figures. Between them are three small objects that may represent the trays and dishes of a banquet. In the lower right is a horse with arched tail. It is difficult to imagine what the projection above his shoulders represents unless it be some type of saddle. Balancing the horse is a peacock(?) in the right corner.

32.   Size: 15 × 87 in. (38 × 220 cm.)
Location: Cave IX (43)
Tile ends and beam ends, indicating the eaves of a roof. A large number of the vestibules and caves at Chiating have tile-end designs over the entrances to indicate a roof. But most of them are in exposed positions and consequently are very badly weathered; these tile ends, in a protected rear corner of a large vestibule, are in very good condition and show typical Han dynasty designs. The same or similar designs can be found in any of the numerous Chinese works on tiles of this period. The two designs on the beam ends below the tiles are also of considerable interest. The one on the left somewhat resembles rubbings of two Han sundials, one formerly in Tuan Fang's collection and the other now in the Royal Ontario Museum.[1] This design also resembles a maltese or formée cross, as pointed out by Bishop White in a letter on this design, and may in fact be nothing more. The object on the right, if it be other than a geometric pattern, cannot be identified at present. But if the design on the left does indeed represent a sundial, then perhaps the one on the right represents the sun, although this is generally symbolized by the three-legged crow.[2] If the third beam end originally bore a design, it is now unrecognizable.

Baber describes and illustrates a design from a cave near Suifu (i.e., Hsuchow or I-pin) which would be more or less identical with this one were it not for the fact that the Suifu beam ends are undecorated.[3] In the Chiating rubbing, the tile ends and beam ends occur at irregular intervals in relation to one another, and Baber makes an interesting observation on the mathematics of the "disc-and-label" pattern he found at Suifu. He states that every fifth beam end regains vertical coincidence with a tile end, and from this works out a ratio of thirteen to four. Either by coincidence or design, the dimensions of the vestibule in which this pattern occurred were of the same ratio. Without accurate measurements of the Chiating vestibule, which, moreover, is irregular, a similar comparison is unfeasible.

33.   Size: 18 × 44 in. (46 × 110 cm.)
Location: Cave IX (45)
Section of tile ends and beam ends, similar to No. 32, indicating a roof. A *t'ao t'ieh,* or monster mask, under the tiles is typical of others found in Szechwan on Han dynasty *ch'üeh.* See Nos. 60–63.

34.   Size: 12 × 28 in. (30.5 × 70.5 cm.)
Location: Cave VIII (36)
A mask of human appearance but with projections resembling horns. Underneath is a walking dog.

35.   Size: 30½ × 35 in. (78 × 89.5 cm.)
Location: Cave VI (29)
This relief bears some resemblance to a compound or reflex bow. A study of this form has been made by Shang Ch'eng-tso, who is of the opinion that this was intended to represent a roof support (*erh chu*). He presents much evidence, textual and pictorial, to support his thesis.[1] Indeed the same type of support is commonly seen, not only in some Han architecture, but also in present-day China—especially in pailou and temple architecture. Some Han *ch'üeh* still standing in Honan and Szechwan show this support very clearly. It appears in reliefs again centuries later in the great Buddhist cave temples at Yün-kang.[2] See No. 90.

36.　Size: 20 × 24 in. (52.5 × 61 cm.)
Location: Chiating
Endless design of seven loops, similar to the one in the upper right corner of No. 87.

II. Hsinchin

37.　Size: 26¼ × 83½ in. (67 × 211 cm.)
Location: Private collection
A group of seven people. On the left is a woman with a basket gathering fruit or leaves from a tree. Close behind her is a man who seems to be pleading with her. These two figures correspond closely to those of Ch'iu Hu and his wife found on the Wu reliefs.[1] According to the legend connected with these figures, an official, returning home after an absence of five years, encountered a woman picking mulberry leaves. He attempted to become intimate with her but she repulsed him. On reaching his home he learned that she was his own wife, whom he had not recognized because of their separation. In the center two men face each other. The one on the left, perhaps a soldier, holds a malletlike object in his right hand and grasps his sword hilt with his left hand. He is wearing overlapping short skirts and some type of boots or protective leggings. The other person wears a quilted cap, a type frequently seen on Han dynasty tomb tiles from Honan. The remaining three persons are grouped together on the right. The one on the left of this group is standing in a respectful attitude and is holding what appears to be a *kuei*. The other two men face each other and seem to be conversing and grasping hands. The men, with the possible exception of the second from the right, carry swords, and the five civilians are elaborately dressed. This relief and Nos. 48 and 50 are from one side and both ends of the same stone coffer.

38.　Size: 26 × 81 in. (66 × 205 cm.)
Location: Szechwan Provincial Museum
A group of five people. The two on the right are conversing, and the one in the center is holding a parasol or banner on a long staff. The group on the

left is indistinct, but it seems to be composed of two women approaching a gate. The figure on the left, if it be but one person, seems to be wearing a mask. In the upper right corner can be seen objects resembling tail feathers of the phoenix or Red Bird of the South. The woman on the far left seems to be holding similar feathers.[1]

39.　Size: 23 × 83 in. (58.5 × 210 cm.)
Location: Szechwan Provincial Museum
Procession showing an official on his way to take office. The official in the tasseled chariot on the right is preceded by an escort chariot. A horseman at flying gallop leads the procession.[1] Along the route stand people in respectful attitudes.

40.　Size: 24 × 68¼ in. (61 × 170 cm.)
Location: Szechwan Provincial Museum
Three highly animated figures. The more complex of the figures (to the left) appears to be holding some creature with an animallike face or mask. It may also be possible that the animal is in the act of casting off a mask and clothing. This creature and its captor or protector are fleeing from another person with a long lance or sword hot in pursuit. The attitude of the latter closely resembles that of a lunging fencer. The final figure on the right is also in pursuit (of the second figure?) and is brandishing a sword. The horizontal object with diagonal striae may be some kind of shield.[1] See No. 41.

41.　Size: 25 × 80 in. (63.5 × 205 cm.)
Location: Szechwan Provincial Museum
This scene bears a striking resemblance to No. 40, but there are some important differences. At the left, some high personage is seated on a kind of dais watching the action of the other three figures. Here the animal is very clearly depicted and resembles a gibbon or orangutan; the animal is isolated here, whereas in No. 40 it is held by a man. As in the other scene, the animal is being attacked by a man thrusting a weapon at its left eye. Although one of these scenes must have been copied from the other, or both from a common source, the drawing in this one is not so good as that of No. 40, nor is the action

so powerfully portrayed. A similar scene occurs in No. 14. A very interesting combat scene from a Han tomb in Nan-yang bears some similarity to these two Hsinchin reliefs.[1]

42.   Size: $17\frac{1}{2} \times 26\frac{1}{2}$ in. (44.5×68 cm.)
Location: West China Union University
A standing figure holding two objects similar to those frequently seen in the Shantung reliefs. The large object is the same as those seen in rubbings of Han reliefs from Nan-yang which are termed *hsiao*, objects used in dancing, probably to mark the time. Chinese sources also define *hsiao* as a "dancing staff" (*wu kan*). Similarly shaped objects, unidentified by Chavannes, can be seen in the Wu reliefs. However, these are sometimes flexible and often carried by horsemen, so their function may be different. The object held in the man's right hand is called a *fu*, or symbol of authority, by Chavannes in agreement with Chinese archaeologists.[1]

43.   Size: 19×36 in. (49×91.5 cm.)
Location: Szechwan Provincial Museum
Two soldiers or officials conversing. The low-slung swords are very long, but actual Han dynasty swords that have been recovered from tombs are extremely long. See No. 68. Something, which may be a bow case or quiver, protrudes behind the figure on the left. The one on the right is holding some object, perhaps a shield, which seems to be resting on the hilt of his sword.

44.   Size: $28 \times 42\frac{1}{2}$ in. (72×107 cm.)
Location: West China Union University Museum
Portrait of a sitting man.

45.   Size: $26\frac{1}{4} \times 37\frac{1}{2}$ in. (68×94 cm.)
Location: Szechwan Provincial Museum
Sitting man. Both this and the preceding recall some of the Chu Wei figures that appear more like portraits than the stereotyped faces in the Wu reliefs.[1]

46.   Size: 19×19 in. (49×49 cm.)
Location: Szechwan Provincial Museum
A mythical winged horse. The inscription beside it is from a pottery brick found within the stone coffer on which the relief occurs. The inscription reads: "Yung P'ing thirteenth year third month made," corresponding to A.D. 70 and provides a *terminus post quem* if the tile was not inserted at a later date.[1] The tile is $2\frac{1}{4} \times 13$ in. (5.5×33 cm.).

47.   Size: 20×43 in. (50.5×109.5 cm.)
Location: Szechwan Provincial Museum
Spined dragon with a disk resembling a *pi* that appears to be supported by the dragon's exceptionally long tongue. This bears some resemblance to a figure on one of the famous Shen *ch'üeh* in Szechwan, in which a dragon holds in his mouth a ribbon attached to a *pi*.[1]

48.   Size: $26 \times 28\frac{1}{2}$ in. (66×73 cm.)
Location: Private collection
A finely balanced picture of two long-tailed birds on a tree. These probably represent the *feng* and *huang*, mythical birds often called the phoenix, whose appearance is regarded as an auspicious omen. The *feng*, the male, with a long comb, is on the right, and the female on the left. Forgeries of this stone are said to exist. See No. 37.

49.   Size: 21×24 in. (52.5×61 cm.)
Location: Szechwan Provincial Museum
A bird resembling a peacock, probably the *chu ch'io*, the Red Bird, symbol of the South.[1]

50.   Size: 24×29 in. (62×73 cm.)
Location: Private collection
A man standing between two *ch'üeh*, apparently offering some object resembling a bolt of cloth. This combination of a donor and *ch'üeh* also appears in Nos. 87 and 88. See No. 37.

51.   Size: $21 \times 25\frac{1}{2}$ in. (54.5×64 cm.)
Location: Szechwan Provincial Museum
Horse and rider with lance between two *ch'üeh*. Forgeries of this stone are said to exist.

52.   Size: 15¾ × 72 in. (40 × 181 cm.)
Location: Private collection
Two chariots approaching a gateway or a *ch'üeh*
preceded by a man, probably a guard.[1] See No. 53.
The relief has been badly damaged in removing
this side of the coffer.

53.   Size: 19 × 78 in. (49 × 200 cm.)
Location: Szechwan Provincial Museum
A scene similar to No. 52. Here two advance guards
can be seen, but part of the lower one is missing. A
welcoming attendant awaits the arrival of the occu-
pants of the chariots. Cf. No. 39.

54.   Size: 21½ × 78 in. (54 × 198 cm.)
Location: Szechwan Provincial Museum
A rearing dragon surrounded by people and animals. In back of the dragon is a person, who appears to be a divinity, sitting on his legs and
holding some kind of scepter. To the right there is
a group of three standing people, the one on the far
right being almost totally destroyed. These appear
to be an official and his attendants. One attendant
is holding some objects (mirrors?) from which
seem to come zigzag streaks like lightning. This
figure resembles Tien Mu, Goddess of Lightning,
who appears later. It is also possible that the zigzag represents the edge of a cliff or pool. In front
of the dragon is the strange tree of Near Eastern
appearance frequently seen in the Shantung reliefs.
Under the tree are a bird resembling a pheasant,
and a deer that appears to have wings; both are
auspicious omens. Above the deer is part of a very
large bird. Drake mistakes the wings or streamers
frequently seen on Han reliefs of horses or dragons
for "water weeds."[1]

55.   Size: 23 × 82½ in. (57 × 206 cm.)
Location: Szechwan Provincial Museum
A weird plant with peacocks, birds, and an archer.
The twisting, tropical-looking plant is more or less
symetrical and has a large bird resembling a peacock on either main branch. There are twelve
smaller birds scattered over the scene, and below
is an archer about to shoot at one of them. This re-

sembles the legend of Hou Yi shooting down nine
of the ten suns as depicted in the Wu Liang reliefs.
The twelve birds here may represent the twelve
moons that were in the sky before eleven were shot
down.[1]

56.   Size: 22 × 38½ in. (57 × 97 cm.)
Location: Private collection
A large and impressive scene of two spiritual beings
and two men. On the left a large bird on a perch
overlooks the two divinities kneeling on either side
of a gaming board and low table. Both of these
creatures appear to be female, and one of them has
wings. A large, vulturelike bird wings its way
toward the two men. The one on the left is playing
a musical instrument resembling a *ch'in*. The other
figure is not very distinct, but appears to be a man
listening to the performance. Lute (*ch'in*) playing
is represented on some of the Han bricks from Szechwan, but they are obviously festive scenes. But
here there is only one person in the audience, and
this suggests the legend of Po Ya. Po Ya, who is
said to have lived around 700 B.C., played the lute
with supernatural ability and is frequently represented on Han mirrors in company with his teacher
Ch'eng Lien and his great admirer Chung Tzu-ch'i.
Does this scene represent Po Ya with just one other
member of the triad? The legend further states that
Ch'eng Lien transported his pupil to the Isles of
the Immortals to perfect his technique. Perhaps the
whole scene represents teacher and pupil studying
among the celestials.[1] On the far right some mythical beast, probably a winged dragon, balances the
bird on the extreme left.

The game scenes from Szechwan are of interest
because they show details not apparent in the Shantung representations of similar scenes. In this relief
and the more earthly scene from the brick shown
in No. 80 there are game boards with six sticks or
counters on them and in this respect correspond to
the picture of *liu po*, so designated by two accompanying characters, on a Han mirror.[2] The Shantung scenes, similar to but not the same as these two,
have been interpreted as a magical performance,
a feast, and divination.[3] The square object with ge-

ometrical designs on it has been compared to or identified with Han sundials by several scholars.[4] In view of the additional information furnished by the Szechwan reliefs, a review of the problem is planned in a future publication. See No. 57.

57.　Size: 26 × 85½ in. (66 × 217 cm.)
Location: Szechwan Provincial Museum
A gaming scene similar to the left part of No. 56. Two winged deities are engaged in a spirited game; both are probably female, but only the one on the right has well-defined breasts. The work on this stone is better than the preceding, and there are several additions. The gaming equipment is the same, but bowls and ladles, frequently seen in similar scenes in Shantung, are added. Behind the deity on the right is a weird plant somewhat reminiscent of the "calendar plant" of the Wu Liang reliefs. A whim of the rubbing maker has left the faces of the figures lighter than the rest of their bodies. Forgeries of this relief are said to exist. Drake considers this to be a fortune-telling scene and would undoubtedly apply the same theory to our No. 56. He takes the six horizontal marks (counters) on the board to be the *ch'ien* hexagram of the *Yi ching*.[1] In view of the picture on the Han mirror referred to in No. 56, in which a similar scene is clearly labeled *liu po*, we cannot agree with Drake's conclusion.

58.　Size: 23½ × 24 in. (59.5 × 61 cm.)
Location: Szechwan Provincial Museum
Two mythological creatures with human heads and arms but with serpentlike bodies. The one on the right is holding up the sun, symbolized by the crow on the disk. The one on the left is holding the moon; the design in this disk is unclear but appears to be the cassia tree and hare rather than the toad, which is also frequently used. See No. 59.

59.　Size: 24 × 24½ in. (61 × 62 cm.)
Location: Szechwan Provincial Museum
Very similar to the above; here the sun and moon disks are supported by two hands instead of one. These two creatures are undoubtedly Fu Hsi and his consort Nü Kua. They are frequent subjects in early Chinese art and occur three times in the Wu Liang reliefs.[1] The usual representation of these two mythical beings shows Fu Hsi holding aloft a square, and Nü Kua holding a compass. Here these implements have given way to the sun and moon. Sir Aurel Stein gives a similar illustration showing that this motif was used as late as the seventh century by Chinese living in Turfan.[2] This scene has been adequately treated by Chavannes, and additional material may be found in Chinese sources.[3] See No. 99.

60.　Size: 26 × 63¾ in. (66 × 159.5 cm.)
Location: Szechwan Provincial Museum
Mate to No. 60. This bird, standing on two feet, has been slightly damaged and also shows some definite difference in style. The monster mask and ring are essentially the same as in the mate. This and the next pair differ from some Szechwan double-leaf doors (Nos. 68, 70) in that they have reliefs on only one side. (See fig. 4.)

It is worth noting that the confronting birds on this pair of doors bear a certain resemblance to those on the second-century Shen memorial pillars in Szechwan, and that the bird on both the right pillar and door stands on one foot whereas the one on the left pillar and door stands on two feet.[1] In fact the only real difference between the doors and the south faces of the pillars is that the bird on the pillars is separated from the mask and ring by an inscription. Part of a mask can be seen near the base of the left pillar, and there can be no doubt that this mask, like those on the doors, originally held a ring in its mouth (and in the paws of its bandy legs) as noted by the Chinese archaeologist Hung Kua some eight hundred years ago. Such a mask and ring can still be seen at the base of the Feng Huang pillar that is dated A.D. 121 and is also in Szechman.[2]

61.　Size: 26 × 58¾ in. (66 × 150 cm.)
Location: Szechwan Provincial Museum
One of a pair of tomb doors. The Red Bird, or phoenix, standing on top of a monster mask and

ring. This mask and ring differ from the usual type in that the ring is also held by the monster's claws. See No. 61.

62.   Size: 25 × 63 in. (63.5 × 151 cm.)
Location: Szechwan Provincial Museum
Tomb door with a mythological bird standing above a monster mask and ring symbolizing a handle. This mask is exceptional in that it is bearded. Both birds on this pair of doors appear to be dancing.

63.   Size: 24 × 66 in. (61 × 167.5 cm.)
Location: Szechwan Provincial Museum
Mate to No. 62. Similar masks woven in Han textiles have been found by Stein in Central Asia, but on the whole these monster masks add a new type to those usually found on Han objects from other parts of China.[1] (See fig. 5.)

64.   Size: 17½ × 34¼ in. (44 × 87 cm.)
Location: Szechwan Provincial Museum
A stone door showing a woman sitting with her legs tucked under her. This rubbing clearly shows at the top a tongue that was inserted in a hole to keep the slab in place. The inscription reads: "The filial daughter-in-law, Lady Chao, whose style name is Yi-wen." (See fig. 6.) This slab was not designed for free swinging like the four preceding doors which have vertical corner pivots.

65.   Size: 25¾ × 34 in. (64 × 86.5 cm.)
Location: Szechwan Provincial Museum
Mate to No. 64. Two men sitting on their legs on mats; on the right is an object that appears to be drapery. The inscriptions, from right to left, read: "Chao Mai from Nan-ch'ang, of undetermined style name," and "The worthy son, Chao the official, named Yuan-kung."

Judging from the figures and the language of the inscriptions, we suppose that Chao Mai's wife was still living (or buried elsewhere), that Lady Chao was his daughter-in-law, possibly the wife of his son Yuan-kung, and that the latter was childless, thus causing the doors to be designed by other relatives. Barring the remote possibility of *wei ting*

being a style name, we must conclude that Chao Mai was of such humble origin that he was "of undetermined style name." The figures on both of these slabs suggest a conscious attempt at portraiture. (See photograph of the original, fig. 7.)

66.   Size: 28 × 41 in. (72 × 103 cm.)
Location: West China Union University Museum
Two men, probably servants, carrying large, flat objects. They are walking in front of, or coming out of, what appears to be a cave entrance. The rectangle with a circle in the middle, based on the cash motif, which is above the head of the man on the left, is frequently seen at the entrances to cave tombs at Chiating. (See No. 28.) Above this symbol can be seen a peaked roof with tile ends. This is typical decoration for cave entrances at Chiating. This rubbing was made from a tomb door, and the projection at the top center is designed to fit in a hole in the cave roof and block the shaft.

67.   Provenance: Hsinchin
Size: 19¼ × 36 in. (50.5 × 91.5 cm.)
Location: West China Union University Museum
A mythical bird standing on a mask and ring. The mask, although not very distinct, appears to have a pointed face, human ears, and long, blunt horns. The pivot in the lower left corner can be clearly seen; the upper one has been broken off.

III. Chengtu and Lu Shan Reliefs

68.   Provenance: 5 *li* north of Chengtu
Size: 20 × 45 in. (50 × 115.5 cm.)
Location: Private collection
Tomb door decorated with a guardian, similar to those found on tomb bricks called *t'ing chang* from the characters often found associated with them,[1] armed with a very long sword and a weapon on a long staff resembling a *chi*. Under the guardian's extended arms is the conventional animal mask with ring, frequently seen on Han bronzes, indicating a handle. The sword here is of interest because of its length. Mathematically the sword, from

pommel to scabbard tip, is a quarter less than the height of the man (27.36 in.). The same proportion applies to the two men on the left in No. 37 although they are drawn on a smaller scale. It has long been known that swords in ancient China were of extreme length. The *Shih chi* biography of Ching K'o, would-be assassin of the Ch'in king, says that because the king's sword hung vertically (and was so long) he could not draw it (see No. 13). Many Han iron swords about forty-five inches long have been uncovered and described,[2] and all these cases support the hypothesis of the late C. W. Bishop that swords of this length would be so thick and heavy if made of bronze that they would be of no practical value and so must be made of iron.[3] If we apply the ratio determined from these rubbings to life-size proportions, then a man only five feet four inches tall would carry a sword forty-eight inches (121.9 cm.) long, only one and a quarter inches longer than the longest so far recorded. Making allowance for pommel and scabbard tip measured in the rubbings, the length of the theoretical sword would be just about the same as the longest real one. We may apply Bishop's hypothesis here and say that the swords in Nos. 37 and 68 are made of iron.

From this rubbing we can also clearly see how the scabbard was hung. The jade *porte-épée* is attached to a rather loose belt. The top of the scabbard is not visible, but it is probable that the *porte-épée* is attached close to its center.

69. Provenance: 5 *li* north of Chengtu
Size: 21½ × 46 in. (34.5 × 116.5 cm.)
Location: Private collection
Reverse of No. 68. A horned and winged dragon, apparently in flight. Under it is the mask-and-ring handle, with the ring intersected by the dragon's tail.

70. Provenance: 5 *li* north of Chengtu
Size: 20½ × 38½ in. (52 × 97.5 cm.)
Location: Private collection
Mate to No. 68. The guardian, whose right side is presented here, is clothed in the same type of cos-

tume as the one in No. 68. The upper right corner has been broken off, so the blade of the weapon upon which he is leaning cannot be seen; the handle extends through the mask and ring. His sword, as in No. 68, is slung on his left side, but slung from the belt on his right side there is a short sword or dagger. It has a ring on the butt end of the hilt, typical of swords of this period, and is apparently in a scabbard. Of particular interest is the four-character inscription below his belt and in front of the short sword, rarely seen in this type of relief. Unfortunately it is not clear enough to read with certainty. The object on which the inscription appears hangs from his belt and is probably a pouch of some kind. It resembles a similar object, also associated with a dagger on a Baba figure of uncertain date, found by J. G. Andersson in Inner Mongolia.[1]

71. Provenance: 5 *li* north of Chengtu
Size: 16 × 40 in. (40 × 102 cm.)
Location: Private collection
Reverse of No. 70. A springing or flying beast resembling a tiger with wings or streamers. The upper left corner, including the animal's forepaws, is wanting. As in the other three reliefs of this set of four, there is an animal mask with ring to indicate a handle. The rings on the sides with animals (Nos. 69 and 71) appear to be held by short legs attached to the masks, as on other Szechwan doors (Nos. 60–63). However, the masks and rings on the sides of these two doors with human figures are of the conventional type.

72. Provenance: Lu Shan, Sikang
Size: 22½ × 53 in. (56 × 133 cm.)
Location: *In situ*
A magnificent tiger from one side of a stone coffin. This is the *pai hu* or White Tiger that corresponds to the West, according to early Chinese cosmology. A part of the tiger's long, arched tail is missing because of damage to the stone. See Nos. 73–75 for rubbings of reliefs on the other sides of this sarcophagus.

73. Provenance: Lu Shan, Sikang
Size: 22 × 46½ in. (55 × 121 cm.)
Location: *In situ*
A very dynamic dragon with three spines on the opposite side of the coffin. This is the *ch'ing lung* or Azure Dragon corresponding to the East.

74. Provenance: Lu Shan, Sikang
Size: 13¾ × 15¼ in. (35 × 38 cm.)
Location: *In situ*
A snake and tortoise, symbol of the North, the region of the *hsüan wu* or Somber Warrior; apparently from the northern end of the coffin.

75. Provenance: Lu Shan, Sikang
Size: 18¾ × 32 in. (48 × 65 cm.)
Location: *In situ*
By elimination, this rubbing must be from the south end of the coffin and should represent the *chu ch'io*, the Red Bird of the South. However, in its place is a very interesting picture of a winged divinity holding up an inscription for the observer's benefit. The inscription of thirty-five characters is dated 211 and reads: "The deceased Steward of Accounts, Wang Hui, Po-chao, died in the last decade of the ninth month of the sixteenth or *hsin mao* year of the Chien An period. He was buried on the *chia wu* day of the sixth month of the seventeenth year. Oh! Alas!"

The use of the more complicated *shih* character ("to collect"), frequently used for "ten" in accounts, in place of the normal character of two strokes is generally considered to be a relatively late practice. But since there is no doubt about the authenticity of this relief, we know that these characters were interchanged early in the third century. The addition of the determinative for "heart" to *ai* ("to pity"), as in the penultimate character, now not commonly used, was a fusion current in the latter Han period.[1]

RELIEFS ON BRICK AND TILE

IV. Szechwan Province

76. Provenance: Chengtu, Ting chia yao tien
Size: 18⅛ × 16½ in. (46 × 42 cm.)
Location: Private collection, Chengtu
A rural scene. In the upper register are two dynamic figures of hunters with their bows drawn to the full and about to let fly at geese overhead. Ducks (or geese) and water lilies are shown on the surface of the water, and three very large fish give depth to it. In the lower register five men are harvesting grain, two of them reaping it with scythes. A sixth figure, entering the scene from the left, is bringing food to the laborers, reminiscent of the passage in *Meng Tzu* describing the bringing of food to the workers in the fields.[1] The objects beside each of the bowmen are unclear. On the original brick each object is supported by short legs, which are not clear in the rubbing. (See fig. 8.)

77. Provenance: Chengtu, Ting chia yao tien
Size: 18⅛ × 16½ in. (46 × 42 cm.)
Location: Private collection, Chengtu
A festive scene. In the upper half there are four people sitting on mats in front of low tables. Three of them are listening to the fourth playing on the *ch'in*, an instrument of five or seven strings with a long wooden sounding board. Below is a dancer wearing a trailing gown with long sleeves. The other person standing on a mat in the lower left is either a dancer or a musician playing the drum (cf. No. 78) on the floor near the food containers. Apparently the drum was necessary accompaniment for the dance, even in Han times.[1]

78. Provenance: Chengtu, Ting chia yao tien
Size: 18¼ × 16½ in. (46.5 × 42 cm.)
Location: Private collection, Chengtu
A similar scene showing two couples, who appear to be musicians, with jugglers and dancers. One juggler performing with a number of balls is reminiscent of a similar scene in the Hsiao-t'ang Shan reliefs.[1] The other juggler seems to be brandishing

a sword or stick in his right hand and balancing a vase on his left elbow.[2] Action is well depicted in the animated dancing scene covering the lower right part of the brick. On the left is a posturing man with bare arms facing a whirling female dancer with long sleeves. In his right hand he holds some object with which he is probably beating the drum on the floor near his feet. A man in a similar pose and holding what looks like the same object appears on one of the Nan-yang stones of Han date.[3] He is beating a large horizontal drum on a stand supported by a crouching tiger. The objects under the dancer's feet may be drums with which she is marking time in accordance with the quotation cited in No. 77. Scattered about the floor are mats and food vessels.

79.   Provenance: Chengtu, Ting chia yao tien
Size: 17¾ × 16¼ in. (45 × 41.5 cm.)
Location: Private collection, Chengtu
A banquet scene. Seven people are seated on mats around low tables. The central figure, probably the guest of distinction, is being offered food and drink by two attendants on either side. On the left there are two other guests and on the right another guest and the host, who is sitting near the utensils in the lower part of the picture. This and the two preceding reliefs recall similar scenes in the Wu Liang Tz'u and Chu Wei reliefs in Shantung.[1] These scenes on the Szechwan bricks show garments in clearer detail than other sources and provide supplementary material to studies that already have been made on early Chinese dress.[2]

80.   Provenance: Hsinchin, Pao-tzu Shan
Size: 18¾ × 14¼ in. (46 × 36 cm.)
Location: Hsi-ch'eng Museum, Chengtu
Four kneeling figures enjoying a spirited game and feast. On the board at the lower edge of the picture are six sticks. The scene thus corresponds to the four-party game of *liu po* on the Han mirror referred to in No. 56.

81.   Provenance: P'eng-hsien, Chin-ch'ih-p'u
Size: 17¾ × 9¾ in. (45 × 25 cm.)
Location: Private collection, Chengtu
A person, probably a dancer, standing under the eaves of a tiled roof with two posturing figures on either side. The person in the center is wearing a gown with long and very wide sleeves and has both arms extended. The crouching figure on the far left appears to be holding some malletlike object, while the one on the right is brandishing two swords or wands. The object below his raised right foot is probably a drum. See Nos. 77 and 78.

82.   Provenance: Chengtu, Ting chia yao tien
Size: 18⅛ × 16¼ in. (46 × 41.5 cm.)
Location: Private collection, Chengtu
A high-wheeled chariot with parasol bearing two men, drawn by a sprightly horse and followed by a rider. The scroll (*p'an ch'ih wen*) at the top resembles those on the Szechwan *ch'üeh* of Kao Yi (A.D. 209), and is also similar to those on some Chou and Han bronzes.[1]

83.   Provenance: P'eng-hsien, Chin-ch'ih-p'u
Size: 17½ × 9¾ × 2½ in. (44.5 × 25 × 6.5 cm.)
Location: Private collection, Chengtu
A two-wheeled covered cart similar to those in use in north China today. The horse has a clipped mane, and details of the harness are clearly shown.

84.   Provenance: Szechwan
Size: 15¾ × 3½ in. (40 × 9 cm.)
Location: West China Union University Museum
This brick, although badly damaged, is extremely interesting because it shows the rare combination of two horses in tandem harness drawing an equally rare four-wheeled vehicle. Nothing similar to this can be found in a special study on early Chinese vehicles.[1] The two parallel lines extending from the yoke on the lead horse back to the cart must represent shafts or traces, one on either side of the horses; but here, perhaps as an aid to perspective, the one on the far side of the horses is shown as an unbroken line. This shaft—the far one—is also drawn above the near shaft in keeping with the

practice in Han art of indicating depth by placing distant objects above near objects. The horses are crudely drawn, and the neck and the head of the leading horse are out of proportion to the rest of its body.

85.   Provenance: Kuang-han, Chou-ts'un
Size: 16¼ × 9½ in. (41 × 24 cm.)
Location: Hsi-ch'eng Museum, Chengtu
Two archers mounted on splendid horses with thin legs and cropped manes. Bow and quiver can be seen projecting backward.

86.   Provenance: Chengtu
Size: 18 × 16 in. (46 × 41 cm.)
Location: Hsi-ch'eng Museum, Chengtu
A splendid example of Han architectural detail. On either side of a door stand two very clearly defined memorial pillars called *ch'üeh*. The door itself apparently consists of two double leaves; one of them cannot be seen because it has been shoved all the way open and only its vertical edge faces the viewer. The mythological *feng huang*, commonly called a phoenix in the West, is perched above the doorway. The whole structure is covered by tiled roofs. What at first glance appear to be flying buttresses may be called supplementary *ch'üeh*. In Chinese these are called *tzu ch'üeh*.[1]

87.   Provenance: Chengtu, Ting chia yao tien
Size: 18¼ × 16½ in. (46.5 × 41.5 cm.)
Location: Private collection, Chengtu
A single *ch'üeh* similar to those shown in No. 86. There are two attendants on either side. One is in a welcoming attitude and seems to be offering something to the arriving guest. The other appears to be a guardian and resembles the *t'ing chang* so frequently found on Han bricks from Honan, although the latter generally have the characters for this office alongside the figure.[1] Hanging from the upper tiled roof are two small mythological figures similar to those seen about the roofs of dwellings in the Wu Liang reliefs.[2] The design in the upper right corner may be the Pleiades, indicating location. (See fig. 9.)

88.   Provenance: Chao-hua
Size: 8¼ × 3½ in. (21 × 8.8 cm.)
Location: Private collection, Chengtu
A person in a two-wheeled chariot approaching a *ch'üeh*. This chariot has a well-supported roof lined with tassels instead of the simpler parasol on a single support. The *ch'üeh* closely resembles the one in No. 87. A further parallel is the attendant to the right holding a long horizontal object.

89.   Provenance: Hsinchin
Size: 13¼ × 2¾ × 4¾ in. (33 × 12 × 7 cm.)
Location: Private collection, Chengtu
An official in a chariot approaches from the left preceded by a horseman. Two figures are shown standing in front of the twin *ch'üeh* bowing and welcoming the newcomer. They are holding objects that may be gifts or badges of office.

This brick is of particular interest for two reasons. In the first place, the horseman, somewhat damaged in this brick, is making a reverse shot with bow and arrow toward the chariot behind him. This can be seen very clearly on several similar bricks in the West China Union University Museum of Archaeology. In the second place, the existence of a closely similar scene is of importance. There are the same figures and objects on both bricks, they are in the same positions and attitudes, and the bricks are of about the same size.[1] In spite of the similarity, there are some interesting differences in detail. The chariots are of the same general type, but the first has wheels of eight spokes; the second has sixteen spokes in each wheel. Both horses in the first brick are rather realistic, but the horses in the second brick, especially the one pulling the chariot, are long-necked, thin-limbed, and in general have a mythical, unearthly quality about them. The *ch'üeh* also differ markedly; those in the first brick are tall, narrow, and close together; those in the second are squat and farther apart. We are at a loss to explain the significance of the horseman's shooting at the chariot he should be escorting. Is this merely a decorative scene, copied by one artisan from another, or was it thus widely used because of the importance of its meaning?

34

90. Provenance: Szechwan
Size: 20 × 5¾ × 3½ in. (50.8 × 14.5 × 9 cm.)
Location: West China Union University Museum
An ox-drawn cart approaching a house. One man is walking beside the ox, and another precedes it. The two-storied house is built on stilts, and entrance is gained by means of a ladder, the lower level being considerably higher than the man standing underneath it. The positions of the ox and men indicate that the house was not built on piles because of marshy ground or water. We have been unable to find other Han illustrations of this type of structure, which bears some resemblance to the "long-house" of southern China.[1] The two U-shaped objects under the eaves are probably *erh chu* supports for the tiled roof. The West China Union University Museum has model houses of baked clay found in Szechwan tombs of the Han date which show clearly this support in the same position.[2] Other examples of the *erh chu* support can be seen in existing Han memorial pillars in Szechwan.[3] (See No. 35.) In this rubbing, as in the original brick, the object above the ox is unclear.[4]

The rubbing also includes the edge of the brick, which in our illustration begins just under the wheels and the house supports. This edge clearly shows the method used for locking bricks together without mortar. The white strip between the black ones represents a groove down the center of the edge made to receive a projecting rib of another brick, thus utilizing the same principle as the tongue and groove so common in our woodwork. On either end of the edge can be seen projections on opposite corners, the one on the right end being somewhat damaged. These are designed to fit into the corresponding grooves of the adjacent bricks, thus locking it into place. In this manner four of the six surfaces of the bricks are used to anchor them.

91. Provenance: Ch'iung-lai, Hua-p'ai-fang
Size: 18 × 14 in. (45 × 34.5 cm.)
Location: Hsi-ch'eng Museum, Chengtu
A pictorial representation of the salt industry that has existed in Szechwan from ancient times. On the left can be seen a derrick erected over a salt-brine well, with four men standing on scaffolding and hauling up brine from the well below with the aid of a windlass or pulleys. To the right of the second stage of the scaffolding can be seen a hopper on props; the brine is poured into it and then conducted by pipes to the evaporating pans in the lower right. The pipes used for this purpose today are of bamboo, and undoubtedly the same material was used in Han times. One man, standing, is watching the pans while a second, kneeling, is tending the fire of the long oven. The rest of the picture shows a hunting scene. In the upper right two men under a tree are shooting, apparently with crossbows, at an animal on the mountain side. Winding from the salt well on the lower left and leading up and to the right is a line that appears to be a mountain path with several people walking along it. See No. 92.

An early geography of this area records the drilling of twenty salt wells in 67 B.C. at the same town where this brick was found.[1]

92. Provenance: Chengtu
Size: 18½ × 16½ in. (47 × 42 cm.)
Location: Private collection, Chengtu
Another salt-making scene with the same general arrangement as No. 91. This brick clearly shows the conduit leading from the derrick to the oven holding five evaporating pans. Two men bearing burdens, probably packs of salt, are walking along the foot of the third hill from the left. Again there is a hunting scene, with two hunters in the upper right stalking two deer. The upper right part of this brick has been lost, but it probably contained more of the hunting scene.

The process depicted in these two rubbings is essentially the same as that employed at Tzuliuching and other places in Szechwan today except that steam winches are used for hauling up the brine, and natural gas, a by-product of the industry, is used to heat the evaporating ovens. In No. 92 the four straight lines leading into the mouth of the oven look more like gas conduits than fuel. Moreover, the elevation of each pan as it recedes from the mouth of the oven also suggests the use of nat-

35

ural gas as fuel. This same arrangement is found necessary today in order to force the gas, lighter than air, to the far end of the long oven.[1] Moreover, the fourth-century geography referred to in No. 91 clearly states that during Han times gas from "fire wells" was used for evaporating the brine. A work on Chinese industries published in 1637 contains a complete description of the process and good woodblock illustrations showing in detail the scenes depicted in these bricks.[2]

The use of the hillocks in these two reliefs gives a feeling of depth and perspective not often encountered in Han reliefs.

93.   Provenance: Kuang-han, Chou-ts'un
Size: 18½ × 10½ in. (47 × 27 cm.)
Location: Hsi-ch'eng Museum, Chengtu
A market scene. Apparently the entrance to this market place is through the two-story building in the lower right corner. This is marked with the two characters *shih lou* ("market tower"), and two people, probably bartering, are on the ground floor. There is an unidentifiable object apparently suspended from the beams of the top roof; this object seems to be cylindrical and may be a drum, indicating that this structure was also used as a drum tower. A large bird is perched on the uppermost tiled roof. The open area of the market is occupied by three pairs of people buying and selling various goods. A restaurateur is shown beside his covered stove in the lower left corner. At the left end of this brick is shown a large double-leafed gate; the three characters above it, *tung shih men*, indicate that this is the "east market gate."[1]

94.   Provenance: Ch'iung-lai, Hua-p'ai-fang
Size: 11½ × 15 in. (29.5 × 38 cm.)
Location: Private collection, Chengtu
A strange birdlike creature with human head; its body is the symbol of the moon. The cassia tree and toad, two of the three symbols commonly shown in the moon disk, are very clearly represented; the third, the hare preparing the elixir of immortality with mortar and pestle, is not shown. This creature has a headdress or coiffure resembling a hat, and

six stars are shown in the background. A Han relief found in Nan-yang, Honan, shows a legendary four-limbed being with human face and serpentlike body holding a lunar symbol that is also combined with six stars.[1]

Another brick bearing an almost identical figure that represents the sun has been found in the same place. The disk in the center of its body contains a bird. It is seen from above and the legs are not visible, but it is undoubtedly the three-legged crow, symbol of the sun. Seven stars are shown in the background.[2] See No. 95.

95.   Provenance: Chengtu, Ting chia yao tien
Size: 12¼ × 16 in. (31 × 40.5 cm.)
Location: Private collection, Chengtu
This is another birdlike creature with human face, but the wings are more stylized than the preceding two and no body, except the disk, is shown. There is probably a sun or moon symbol on the disk, but it is not distinct in this rubbing.

Although the sun and moon disks occur in other Han reliefs from various parts of China, we believe the solar and lunar winged beings shown in these three rubbings to be unique and suggest that they show Taoist or outside influence. An analogous bird with a disk body occurs in the Nan-yang reliefs and there appears to be some design on the disk, but in its present state it is illegible. Sun Wen-ch'ing, who has studied the Nan-yang reliefs, considers it to be the Red Bird, symbol of the South, but it may be a lunar or solar symbol similar to the ones presented here.[1]

Fischer illustrates a painted brick showing a creature similar to those from Szechwan. Although shown in profile, in some respects it bears a close resemblance to the latter. The headdress is the same as that in No. 95, which differs radically from the other two Szechwan examples. Fischer places this painting between the fourth and fifth centuries. He compares the head ornament to a cock's comb and says that this plus the predominant red color and the "tongues of flame" suggest a fire spirit.[2]

Lacking authenticated examples identical with ours but relying upon the Nan-yang examples and oral evidence obtained in Chengtu, we tentatively date these three bricks (Nos. 94, 95, and the similar one in *Shu chuan chi*) as late Han.

96.   Provenance: Hsinchin, Pao-tzu Shan
Size: 15¾ × 2½ × 4¾ in. (40 × 7 × 12 cm.)
Location: West China Union University Museum
Hsi Wang Mu with attendants. The so-called Queen Mother of the West is seated on a throne formed by the backs of two animals with extended forelegs. They resemble a dragon and a tiger, perhaps symbolizing East and West. This type of throne occurs rarely in Han art from other parts of China but is very common in Szechwan.[1] On the left is the hare pounding the drug of immortality, symbol of the moon; he appears to be aided by an unrecognizable kneeling figure, possibly the toad, another moon symbol. Approaching Hsi Wang Mu from the left is an attendant who is offering her a branch. To the right of her throne is the three-legged bird, symbol of the sun, and the bushy- or nine-tailed fox, an auspicious omen. See No. 97.

97.   Provenance: Hsinchin
Size: 15¾ × 2½ × 4¾ in. (40 × 7 × 12 cm.)
Location: West China Union University Museum
Essentially the same as No. 96 but with a slightly different arrangement of figures. Here we see two persons entering the scene from the left, the three-legged bird, an attendant making an offering, Hsi Wang Mu on the same strange throne, the nine-tailed fox, and finally the lunar hare preparing the drug of immortality. Great numbers of these two bricks have been found in Szechwan.

Scenes of Hsi Wang Mu are well known through the published reliefs of the Wu Liang offering shrine in Shantung, but they differ from these bricks in that in the former she is not accompanied by the nine-tailed fox, the three-legged crow, and the lunar hare. Other Shantung and Honan reliefs bear a closer resemblance to the scenes under discussion as pointed out by Chavannes.[1]

98.   Provenance: Kuang-han
Size: 10½ × 3¼ × 14¾ in. (26.5 × 8.5 × 37.5 cm.)
Location: Hsi-ch'eng Museum, Chengtu
One end of this brick shows three mythological beings, one with a bird perched on his arm. The other end bears an inscription of four characters evenly divided into two groups; each group is in the loop of a sort of figure-eight design composed of circles and squares. The inscription reads "Yung Yuan, eighth year." This corresponds to A.D. 96 and the eighth year of the reign of Emperor Ho of the Later Han dynasty. The largest areas, the sides and edges, are undecorated. The designs are based on the cash motif and are frequently seen on Han bricks. Sometimes the round object that divides the inscription in this rubbing has a square hole and bears characters found on coins of that period.[1] A similar brick has been found in P'eng hsien. On it three mythological beings are in the reverse order and there is no inscription at the other end.[2]

99.   Provenance: Kuang-han
Size: 3 × 32½ in. (7.5 × 83 cm.)
Location: West China Union University Museum
Sun, moon, and other symbols from the top of an arc of baked clay. On the right a disk with a bird, representing the sun, is held aloft by a creature with a human face and arms and a serpent's body. Below it is a figure resembling a bird. At the end is a tortoise, representing the North. On the left is a similar being supporting the moon disk with the toad in it. An indeterminate figure is beside it, corresponding to the bird on the other half. Below it is the *chu ch'io*, or Red Bird of the South. Each panel is terminated by the chevron design at either end frequently seen on Han bricks. These beings, as those in Nos. 58 and 59, are derived from Fu Hsi and Nu Kua.[1]

These mold-made bricks are used to cover the top of a coffin, and are made so that their sides form a tongue-and-groove joint. The brick is about seven inches wide at the greatest height of the arc, where the two chevron patterns oppose each other, and tapers down to about two inches at the ends. A photograph of three of these dovetailed together (ridge along one side and groove on the other) has been published.[2]

100.   Provenance: P'eng Shan
Size: 17 × 11 in. (44 × 28 cm.)
Location: Szechwan Provincial Museum
An oblong brick, with diaper-pattern border, showing mythological and other scenes. On the left are two earthly scenes of a rider and a chariot. In the upper right is the now familiar figure of Hsi Wang Mu on her dragon-tiger throne (see Nos. 96 and 97). Below is the nine- or bushy-tailed fox, an auspicious omen, probably the lunar hare pounding the drug of immortality, and other symbolical figures. The four panels have the appearance of having been stamped into wet clay with sectional dies.

Academica Sinica excavated many P'eng Shan tombs a few years ago under the direction of G. D. Wu (Wu Chin-ting), but the material was not published before his recent death and probably never will be.

NOTES

I

NTRODUCTION

[1] Edouard Chavannes, *La Sculpture sur pierre en Chine au temps des deux dynasties Han* (Paris, 1893), and *Mission archéologique dans la Chine septentrionale.* I, 1, *La Sculpture a l'époque des Han*, Paris, 1913. Sekino Tei, *Shina santōshō ni okeru kandai fumbo no hyōshoku*, Tōkyō, 1916.

[2] *Chung kuo hui hua shih*, vol. 1, pp. 15–24, perhaps gives the most complete list; some Western writers have also quoted some of these sources. See note 13.

[3] Arthur Waley, *The Temple and Other Poems*, pp. 95–97.

[4] *Han wu liang tz'u hua hsiang lu*, vol. 2, fol. 37 a–b.

[5] Chinese textiles of the Han period formed one of the main items of export, and numerous examples of them have been preserved in the dry climates of Central Asia and the Near East. Since many of them were especially designed for foreign trade, Western art motifs were consciously brought into China and copied for this purpose. On this subject see Maenchen-Helfen, "From China to Palmyra," *Art Bulletin*, vol. 25 (1943), 358–362; Lopez, "Silk Industry in the Byzantine Empire," *Speculum*, vol. 20 (1945), 1–42; Simmons, *Chinese Patterned Silks*; and Trever, *Excavations in Northern Mongolia*.

[6] The tomb and frescoes are described by Hamada Kosaku, *Tōa kōkogaku kenkyū*, pp. 421–427. A more detailed description of the paintings with line drawings of them is in Yagi's *Manshū kōkogaku*, pp. 287–326.

[7] Mori Osamu, *Ying-ch'eng-tzu*, p. 35, fig. 34.

[8] Many reproductions of this tray may be found in works on Chinese art, including Fischer, *Die chinesische Malerei der Han-Dynastie*, pl. 58, but the best are those in the official report of the excavation. See Harada, *Lo-lang*, pls. 56–59, where this painting is reproduced in color.

[9] See Harada, *op. cit., passim.* A detailed study of dated Han dynasty lacquer has been made by Umehara in his *Shina kandai kinenmei shikki zusetsu*. Beginning with three lacquer pieces dated 85 B.C. that were found in northern Korea (pls. 1 ff. and pp. 6 ff.), he describes and illustrates more than thirty inscribed and dated lacquer objects made in Szechwan during the Early and Late Han periods.

[10] For reproductions of these frescoes see the official report on the excavation, Mori Osamu, *Ying-ch'eng-tzu*, pls. 36–45.

[11] Details of these paintings in color and in black and white may be seen in *Rakurō saikyō tsuka*, the official report on this tomb compiled by the Chōsen Koseki Kenkyū Kwai, pls. A and 43–50.

[12] Reproductions of some of these paintings are given in all modern works on early Chinese art. The official illustrations, all in black and white, are in Tomita, *Portfolio of Chinese Paintings in the Museum*, pls. 1–8. An excellent color reproduction of one of the tiles appears as the first plate (unnumbered) in Fischer, *Die chinesische Malerei der Han-Dynastie*.

[13] More or less complete surveys of the art of this period appear in a number of works on Chinese art. Some of the more useful ones are Fischer, *Die chinesische Malerei der Han-Dynastie*; Siren, *A History of Early Chinese Painting*, vol. 1, and *A History of Early Chinese Art*, vols. 2, 3; Waley, *An Introduction to the Study of Chinese Painting*; Bachhofer, *A Short History of Chinese Art*; and Soper, "Early Chinese Landscape Painting," *Art Bulletin*, vol. 23 (1941), 141–164. A popular and profusely illustrated account is given in Dagny Carter, *Four Thousand Years of China's Art* (New York, 1948), pp. 64–92. The best survey of Han painting for the time it was written (1932), and the only one that takes into account all of the actual paintings then known is Hamada's "Kandai no kaiga ni

oite," in Mori, *Ying-ch'eng-tzu*, pp. 39–44. I have been unable to see Acker, "On the Painting of the Han Period," *Memoirs of the Research Department of the Toyo Bunko*, vol. 8, 33–44, which is a translation of Hamada's article.

No attempt has been made in this brief survey of Han art to include all recent finds pertinent to the subject. For such material the reader should consult Umehara Sueji, *Tōa kōkogaku gaikan*, Kyōto, 1947. This work, not available to me, has one section dealing with the work of Japanese archaeologists in China up to 1944.

[14] *Szu ch'uan ku tai wen hua shih*, p. 16. See also the first chapter of this work for the prehistory of Szechwan.

[15] Feng Han-yi, "The Megalithic Remains of the Chengtu Plain," *Journal of the West China Border Research Society*, vol. 16 (1945), ser. A, 15–22.

[16] Ségalen, text and pls. XV–LV; Chavannes, p. 8 ff.

[17] On the early communications and intercourse of the Szechwan region, see *Szu ch'uan ku tai wen hua shih*, pp. 112–119.

[18] Bishop, "The Problem of the Min River Caves," *Chinese Social and Political Science Review*, vol. 10 (1926), 46–61. Ségalen, *op. cit., passim*.

[19] Ségalen, *op. cit.*, pp. 145 ff.

[20] Torrance, "Burial Customs in Sz-chuan," *Journal of the North China Branch of the Royal Asiatic Society*, vol. 41 (1910), 57–75. Graham, "The Ancient Caves of Szechwan Province," *Proceedings of the United States Museum*, vol. 80, art. 16 (1932).

[21] For details of the Shantung shrines see Wilma Fairbank, "The Offering Shrines of 'Wu Liang Tz'u,'" *Harvard Journal of Asiatic Studies*, vol. 11 (1941), 1–36. A good view of the interior of a loggia of the same type as those at Chiating is shown in Ségalen, pl. LXVI.

[22] "Ssu ch'uan hsin chin teng ti han yai mu k'ao lüeh," *Chin-ling hsüeh pao*, vol. 10 (1940), 1–18.

[23] Shang Ch'eng-tso, *op. cit.*; Laufer, "Chinese Sarcophagi," *Ostasiatische Zeitschrift*, vol. 1 (1912–1913), 318–334, considered these to be actual sarcophagi.

[24] A good illustration of one of the coffers with relief can be seen in Ségalen, pl. LXVII. The same illustration, in reduced scale, appeared earlier in Ségalen, "Premier exposé des résultats archéologiques obtenus dans la Chine occidentale," *Journal Asiatique*, vol. 6 (1915), ser. 11, fig. 8.

[25] Shang Ch'eng-tso, *op. cit.* See especially D. C. Graham, "Notes on the Han Dynasty Grave Collection in the West China Union University Museum of Archaeology," *Journal of the West China Border Research Society*, vol. 9 (1937), 213–218, and T. Torrance, "Notes on the Cave Tombs and Ancient Burial Mounds of Western Szechwan," *op. cit.*, vol. 4 (1930–1931), 88–96, for descriptions and illustrations.

[26] Wilma Fairbank in her important study, "A Struc-

tural Key to Han Mural Art," *Harvard Journal of Asiatic Studies*, vol. 7 (1932), 52–88, suggests that these were the source of many of the figures on Han reliefs in Shantung. This theory indeed seems plausible and may even be applied to a few of the Hsinchin reliefs, especially the processions. But on the whole the reliefs from Szechwan are characterized by more individuality and life than those from Shantung.

[27] W. C. White, *Tomb Tile Pictures of Ancient China*.

[28] *Han tai k'uang chuan chi lu*, postface, 1a.

[29] Shang ch'eng-tso, "Ssu-ch'uan hsin chin teng ti han yai mu chuan mu k'ao lüeh," *Chin ling hsüeh pao*, vol. 10 (1940), 2, and W. Franke, "Die Han Zeitlichen Felsengraeber bei Chia-ting," *Studica Serica*, vol. 7 (1948), 38–39.

[30] *Li shih*, ch. 13, pp. 9b–10b (*Ssu pu ts'ung k'an* ed.).

[31] Henri Maspero, using the Shantung reliefs as source material, wrote an illuminating account of life in second-century China. See his "La vie privée en Chine a l'époque des Han," *Revue des arts asiatiques*, vol. 7 (1931), 185–201.

[32] As pointed out in some detail in the *Nan yang han hua hsiang hui ts'un*, pp. 4b–6a, by the second century there was a fairly large body of literature available, besides oral tradition, which could and did serve as inspiration and guide for the artists of this time. An account of the attempted assassination was included in the *Shih chi* a century or two before the carving of the Chiating reliefs. This work and exaggerated versions of the attempted assassination must have been available to the artists but it is highly improbable that two artists working independently would attain such coincidence from such accounts. For a comparison of Shantung and Szechwan reliefs of this event see R. C. Rudolph, "Han Tomb Reliefs from Szechwan," *Archives of the Chinese Art Society of America*, vol. 4 (1950).

DESCRIPTIONS OF THE RELIEFS

2 [1] Miss Helen Fernald, Royal Ontario Museum, has pointed out the similarity between this and the sixth-century Chinese Buddhist relief in the University of Pennsylvania Museum which illustrates an episode from the Vessantara Jataka. See her "An Early Chinese Sculpture," *University Museum Bulletin*, vol. 5, no. 2 (1934), 48–53, and pl. 7. A similar scene is on the Shen *ch'üeh*. Ségalen, pl. XXIV.

3 [1] Chavannes, 77, 104: Sekino, 55, 65. (N.B. When references to Chavannes and Sekino are separated by a colon, this indicates that the same material may be found in either source.)

6 [1] *Han tai k'uang chuan chi lu*, ch. 1, 15a; ch. 2, 10b.

7 [1] R. Torii, *Sculptured Stone Tombs of the Liao Dy-*

nasty, pls. 2, 5. The actual wearing of an animal mask apparently has an early origin in China. A Chou dynasty bronze shows a human face surmounted by an animal mask similar to the *t'ao t'ieh*. See Hentze, *Objets rituels, croyances et dieux de la Chine antique et de l'Amérique*, fig. 135, pl. VI, p. 73 ff.

8 [1] Chavannes, 148: Sekino, 171.

[2] Mori Osamu and Naito Hiroshi, *Ying-ch'eng-tzu*, pls. XLIV, XLV. The same is reproduced in Carl Hentze, *Die Sakralbronzen und ihre Bedeutung in den fruehchinesischen Kulturen*, Tafelband, IX:18.

9 [1] A photograph of one can be seen in Graham's paper "Persistence of Custom as Illustrated in the Collection of Han Dynasty Clay Images in the West China Museum," *Journal of the West China Border Research Society*, vol. 6 (1934), 105–106, and also in *Proceedings United States National Museum*, vol. 80, art. 16, pl. 10.

[2] C. Hentze, *Chinese Tomb Figures*; Lo Chen-yu, *Ku ming ch'i t'u lu*; Hamada, *Shina ko minki deisho zusetsu*; Cheng Te-k'un, *Chung kuo ming ch'i*.

13 [1] Chavannes, 113, 123, 75: Sekino, 68, 90, 53.

[2] *Shih chi*, ch. 86. This biography has been translated and the Shantung reliefs commented upon by Bodde, *Statesman, Patriot, and General in Ancient China*, chap. 2.

15 [1] Chavannes, 113, 123, 75: Sekino, 68, 90, 53.

17 [1] See W. P. Yetts, "The Horse: A Factor in Early Chinese History," *Eurasia Septentrionalis Antiqua*, vol. 9 (1934), 1–55. He suggests also that Han artists got many of their horse formulas from Hellenistic areas through the medium of coins decorated with horses.

18 [1] W. C. White, *Tomb Tile Pictures of Ancient China*, pls. XXIX, LVI.

19 [1] *Nan yang han hua hsiang hui ts'un*, nos. 44–49.

20 [1] See pl. VI of Torrance's "Burial Customs in Szchuan," *Journal, North China Branch Royal Asiatic Society*, vol. 41 (1910), 57–75.

23 [1] As can be seen from the photograph of the original relief in fig. 2, the animal in the rubbing is facing in the wrong direction. This is due to a mistake of a rubbing mounter in Chengtu. The paper was so thin, and the ink had been applied so liberally, that it was difficult to tell obverse from reverse and the man inadvertently mounted this rubbing face down.

25 [1] The rubbings published by Chavannes and Sekino show very little of this scene owing to damage of the original. But a rubbing used by Wilma Fairbank in "The Offering Shrines of 'Wu Liang Tz'u,'" *Harvard Journal of Asiatic Studies*, vol. 6 (1941), fig. 2, last scene on second register of central slab, shows all the original but on a small scale. The drawing in *Chin shih so* (*Shih so*, ch. 3, and Chavannes, text, pl. DI, no. 1204) is the clearest available, but not entirely reliable.

26 [1] Graham, "The Ancient Caves of Szechwan Province," *Proceedings of the United States Museum*, vol. 80, art. 16 (1932), fig. 12, gives a reconstruction of this house.

28 [1] Variations of the coin motif were universally used in Han times. Among other works, the *Han tai k'uang chuan chi lu*, ch. 2, p. 20a, illustrates a number of examples. Graham, "Ornamented Bricks and Tiles from Western Szechwan," *Journal of the West China Border Research Society*, vol. 10 (1938), gives numerous examples from this region.

29 [1] A copy of this fresco can be seen in Li Wen-hsin's "Liao yang pei yuan hua pi ku mu chi lüeh," *Bulletin of the Preparatory Committee, National Museum of Shen Yang*, no. 1 (1947). Chao Pang-yen, in his study of Han dynasty sports, illustrates an equestrian example of this sport on a Han relief, *Ch'ing chu ts'ai yüan p'ei hsien sheng liu shih wu sui lun wen chi*, vol. 1, p. 531. See also *Chuan men ming chia*, second series.

32 [1] Published by Liu Fu in his paper "Hsi han shih tai jih kuei," *Kuo li pei ching ta hsüeh kuo hsüeh chi k'an*, vol. 3, pt. 4 (1934). The first rubbing and a photograph of the second dial appear in the study by W. C. White and P. M. Millman, "An Ancient Chinese Sun-dial," *Journal of the Royal Astronomical Society of Canada* (November, 1938), 417–430, pl. XII, and fig. 1.

[2] This design recalls the triquetra or triskelion which in one of its forms—three legs radiating from the center of a disk—has been used as a sun symbol in the Mediterranean and has thus something in common with the three-legged crow in the sun disk. Numerous examples of triquetra are shown by Petrie, *Decorative Patterns of the Ancient World*, in the B and D categories. But the Szechwan design more closely resembles the skirls shown by Petrie, *op. cit.*, PQ 5, 9, PX 1, 8, PY 8, PU 3, 6, 9.

[3] E. C. Baber, *Travels and Researches in the Interior of China*, pp. 136–137, fig. 11.

35 [1] *Chung kuo wen hua yen chiu hui k'an*, vol. 1 (1940), 41–60.

[2] Ségalen, pls. XIV, XX, XXVII, XXX, shows good Han examples of this support on *ch'üeh*, and a rubbing on page 50 of Mizuno, *Unko sekibutsu gun* shows the same design as it appears at Yün-kang. Baber, *op. cit.*, p. 135, was the first to advance the theory that this design represented a roof support.

37 [1] Chavannes, 77: Sekino, 55. See also *Ku lieh nü chuan*, ch. 5. See No. 68 for comments on the swords.

38 [1] Cf. Drake, *Monumenta Serica*, vol. 8 (1943), fig. 31, p. 305.

39 [1] A short time ago the "flying gallop" posture was considered to be a product of the imagination and its presence in Chinese art was taken as evidence of cultural borrowing from Mycenae or Scythia. It has since been

proved that this motif was an independent creation in early China. See W. F. Edgerton, "Two Notes on the Flying Gallop," *Journal of the American Oriental Society*, vol. 56 (1936), 178–188, and Ludwig Bachhofer, *A Short History of Chinese Art* (New York, 1946), p. 91.

40   [1] Drake, *op. cit.*, fig. 29, p. 305.

41   [1] *Nan yang han hua hsiang hui ts'un*, no. 136.

42   [1] *Nan yang han hua hsiang hui ts'un*, nos. 104, 105, 106, 140, 141, and 143. Chavannes, text, p. 162, n. 1.

45   [1] Cf. Fischer, *Die chinesische Malerei der Han-Dynastie*, pls. 32–53.

46   [1] Drake, *op. cit.*, figs. 34, 36, p. 306. A similar inscription where the *p'ing* and *shih* (ten) characters are run together in the same way occurs in the fourth rubbing in *Han wei liu ch'ao chuan wen*. These two characters were there regarded as the single character *p'ing*. If this is a correct interpretation, then our inscription should read "Yung P'ing third year . . ." or A.D. 60.

47   [1] Ségalen, pl. XXIII. Yetts, "Notes on Chinese Roof Tiles," *Transactions of the Oriental Ceramic Society*, 1927–1928, fig. 4B, illustrates a Han tile bearing a dragon with almost identical head and a very long tongue. No. 47 may not be authentic, according to information received from Professor Wen after going to press.

49   [1] Drake, *op. cit.*, fig. 33, p. 306.

52   [1] *op. cit.*, fig. 30, p. 305.

54   [1] *Op. cit.*, fig. 28, p. 305.

55   [1] Chavannes, 77, 107: Sekino, 55, 60. Cf. Drake, *op. cit.*, fig. 27, pp. 304–305. See Maenchen, "Der Schuss auf die Sonnen," *Wiener Zeitschrift für die Kunde des Morgenlandes*, vol. 44 (1936), 80–81, and B. Karlgren, "Legends and Cults in Ancient China," pp. 266, 272.

56   [1] Cf. J. E. Lodge, A. G. Wenley, J. A. Pope, *A Descriptive and Illustrative Catalogue of Chinese Bronzes* (Washington, 1946), p. 79, and mirrors 35.13, 36.4, and 37.15. 35.13 also occurs in S. Umehara, *Kan izen no kokyō no kenkyū*, pl. XXX, no. 2, and he compares it with Han reliefs and also with Han textiles which have been found in northern Mongolia. See Camilla Trever, *Excavations in Northern Mongolia*, and W. P. Yetts, "Discoveries of the Kozlov Expedition," reprint from *Burlington Magazine*, April, 1926.

[2] Yang, "A Note on the so-called TLV Mirrors and the Game Liu-po," *Harvard Journal of Asiatic Studies*, vol. 9 (1945–1947), 202–206.

[3] B. Laufer, *Chinese Grave-Sculptures of the Han Period*, p. 35; Chavannes, text, p. 184; and S. Kaplan, "On the Origin of the TLV Mirror," *Revue des arts asiatiques*, vol. 40 (1937), 21–24, respectively.

[4] Cf. Liu Fu, "Hsi Han tai shih tai ti jih kuei," *Kuo hsüeh chi k'an*, vol. 3, no. 4 (1932), 573–610; Orvar Karlbeck, *Catalogue of the Collection of Chinese and Korean Bronzes at Hallwyl House, Stockholm*, pp. 27–30;

W. C. White, "An Ancient Chinese Sun-Dial," *Journal of the Royal Astronomical Society of Canada*, no. 4 (1938), 417–423, and W. P. Yetts, *The Cull Chinese Bronzes*, pp. 150–165.

57   [1] Drake, *op. cit.*, fig. 32, p. 305.

59   [1] Chavannes, 75, 123, 134: Sekino, 53, 90, 77.

[2] Stein, *Innermost Asia*, vol. 3, pl. CIX.

[3] Chavannes, text, pp. 126–130; *Wu liang tz'u t'ang hua hsiang k'ao* (1926) by Ch'ü Chung-jung; *Han pei lu wen* (1918 ed.) by Ma Pang-yu; *Han wu liang tz'u hua hsiang lu* (1936) by Jung Keng, etc. Numerous examples of similar creatures are found on the Nan-yang reliefs as shown in *Nan yang han hua hsiang hui ts'un*, nos. 3, 53–63, but only one (no. 3) holds a symbol aloft. For a probable Hellenistic origin of this motif see G. Ecke, "Atlantes and Caryatides in Chinese Architecture," *Bulletin of the Catholic University of Peking*, no. 7 (1930), 97.

60   [1] A similar mask and ring executed in bronze in the round is illustrated by A. Salmony in "Le Mascaron et l'anneau dans l'art sur les pendentifs et les appliqués," *Revue des arts asiatiques*, vol. 8 (1934), pl. LVIII–b. He says that it comes from the northern frontiers and shows Luristan influence.

61   [1] Ségalen, pls. XVI–XIX.

[2] *Op. cit.*, p. 59, pls. XVI, XIV.

63   [1] Stein, *Innermost Asia*, vol. 3, pls. XXXVII, XL. These Han textiles show a bandy-legged, three-clawed monster closely related to those on the doors. A classification of monster masks appearing on Han tomb bricks has been made by Wang Chen-to in *Han tai k'uang chuan chi lu*, appendix, p. 2b, and ch. 2, pp. 5b–7a. He distinguishes six different classes of this design according to the type of face and the relation of the ring to the mouth, nose, etc. None of the type shown in our nos. 60–63 and 67 appears among the eight examples illustrated by Wang. These Szechwan types will provide further material for the study of the evolution and migration of this design so ably started by Schuyler Cammann, "Tibetan Monster Masks," *Journal of the West China Border Research Society*, vol. 12 (1940), ser. A, pp. 11–16, and R. J. Charleston, "Han Damasks," *Oriental Art*, vol. 1 (1948), 63–81.

68   [1] W. C. White, *Tomb Tiles of Ancient China*, pls. CXXI, CXXII. *Han tai k'uang chuan chi lu*, ch. 2, pp. 9b–12a. The latter work, supplement pp. 3ab, gives a full explanation of the term.

[2] Janse, "Notes sur quelques épées anciennes trouvées en Chine," *Bulletin of the Museum of Far Eastern Antiquities*, no. 2 (1930), states that the longest, nos. 71 and 94, are of iron and are 97.6 and 97 cm. in length, respectively. Laufer, *Chinese Clay Figures, Part I, Prolegomena on the History of Defensive Armor*, pl. XXI, illustrates an iron sword 117.6 cm., (46¾ in.) long. This does not include pommel or scabbard tip but only the blade and tang.

The Royal Ontario Museum in Toronto has at least ten Han swords (NB 1550, 1559, 1563–1568, 1574–1575) between 41½ and 45¾ inches long, made of iron. None of the bronze swords in Toronto attain this length.

³ Personally described to the Western collaborator some years ago and similarly worded in Bodde, *Statesman, Patriot, and General in Ancient China,* p. 45. An apparent contradiction is seen in Matthias Eder's "Eiserne Degen und Schwerter aus der Han-Zeit," *Monumenta Serica,* vol. 8 (1943), 397, n. 2, where he quotes the description of a bronze sword 43½ inches in length from *An Exhibition of Ancient Chinese Ritual Bronzes Loaned by C. T. Loo & Co.* (Detroit Institute of Arts, 1940), no. 60.

70 ¹ Andersson, "Hunting Magic in the Animal Style," *Bulletin of the Museum of Far Eastern Antiquities,* no. 4 (1932), 221–317, pl. XXXVI.

74 ¹ For a full discussion of this symbol see W. P. Yetts, *The Cull Chinese Bronzes,* pp. 144–148. It seems not to have appeared in the Chou period but occurs very frequently in Han art, and Szechwan examples of this date are discussed by Ségalen, p. 80.

75 ¹ Cf. *Chin shih wen tzu pien yi,* ch. 3. This character, according to Hung Kua's *Li shih,* ch. 17, p. 10b (*Ssu pu ts'ung k'an,* ed.), occurs on another Szechwan monument dated 155. This tomb is described in detail by Jen Nai-ch'iang in two articles "Lu shan hsin ch'u han shih t'u k'ao," and "Pien wang hui shih kuan fou tiao," *K'ang tao yüeh k'an* vol. 4, nos. 6 and 7, vol. 5, no. 1 (1942–1943).

76 ¹ *Meng tzu,* 3, ii, 5 (Legge, *The Chinese Classics,* vol. 2, 272). This passage in turn may be related to an earlier one in the *Shih ching* or *Book of Songs,* 4, i, 3, 6 (Legge, *op. cit.,* vol. 4, 604).

77 ¹ In most Han dancing scenes there is either a large horizontal drum on a stand or a rather flat circular object on the floor about which the dancer performs. This object closely resembles the modern small Chinese drum. At least thirteen dancing scenes with drums occur in the Shantung reliefs: Chavannes, 45, 49, 104, 122, 1151, 1238, 1270: Sekino, 10, 17, 65, 89, 173, 111, 150; Chavannes, 149, 158, 160, 163 and Sekino 110, 147. In two unclear rubbings no drum could be seen. In most of these cases the large drum on a stand is used but does not appear in the four Szechwan dancing scenes (nos. 77, 78, 81, 30–31). The small floor drum appears in three cases. Chavannes, text, p. 185, following the *Shih so,* considers this object to be a cushion. In three reliefs showing orchestras, Chavannes, 49, 122: Sekino, 17, 89, and Sekino, 218, drummers are striking this flat drum. Moreover the first-century poet, Fu Yi in his "Ode on the Dance" (Wu fu) says that the measure of the steps is regulated by the drum, and Li Shan in commenting on this says that the dancers struck the drum with their feet

to mark the tempo. See Chao Pang-yen, *op. cit.,* p. 537.

78 ¹ Chavannes, 49: Sekino, 17.

² Juggling balls and swords seems to have been a common combination at this time. Li Yu, a Han official and poet in his *P'ing lo kuan fu* mentions the "flying balls and dancing swords." And the second-century astronomer-poet, Chang Heng, in his famous "Ode on the Western Capital" (*Hsi ching fu*), speaks in a similar vein. These are quoted in Chao Pang-yen, *op. cit.,* p. 533. No Han reference to vase balancing has been found, but the term *t'i p'ing,* occurring in the list of the amusements seen in the bazaars of Pien-liang (K'ai-feng) in the twelfth-century work *Tung ching meng hua lu,* ch. 5, may possibly refer to this sport.

³ *Nan yang han hua hsiang hui ts'un,* no. 138.

79 ¹ Chavannes, 104: Sekino, 65. Fischer, *Die chinesische Malerei der Han-Dynastie,* pls. 32–35.

² Harada, *Kan rikuchō no fukushoku,* and Eberhard, *Die Mode der Han und Chin Zeit.*

82 ¹ Ségalen, pls. XLVII, XLVIII. Cf. *Shang chou yi ch'i t'ung k'ao,* vol. 1, 99 ff. I am indebted to Mr. Laurence Sickman for bringing the Kao Yi dragon-cloud scroll to my notice.

84 ¹ Harada and Komai, *Shina koki zukō,* pt. 2.

86 ¹ A passage from the *Lai hsiang chi,* quoted in *T'ai p'ing yü lan,* ch. 179, in referring to these says, "The *ch'üeh* each have a *tzu ch'üeh.*" They are set back somewhat from the face of the main *ch'üeh* and have tiled roofs. Similar *ch'üeh,* although not so complex as the Szechwan type, are those at the Wu shrine in Shantung, the T'ai Shih, K'ai Mu and Shao Shih *ch'üeh* in Teng-feng hsien, Honan, and the Kao Yi *ch'üeh* Ya-an hsien, Sikang. Cf. *Shikai bijutsu zenshū,* vol. 3, pls. 108, 109, 110; Chavannes, 1–5, 17–18, 27–29, 56–60.

87 ¹ See no. 68, n. 1.

² To our knowledge the *ch'üeh* on this Szechwan tomb tile is the closest parallel to the controversial illustrations of the two *ch'üeh* of Wang chih-tzu that appear in *Shih so,* ch. 4 (Chavannes, 199). These block prints are said to be copies made from rubbings of the original *ch'üeh.* They dated from the late Han and stood in Szechwan. Although they had fallen centuries ago, some fragments are still preserved. See Chavannes, text, pp. 256–258, and Ségalen, text, pp. 118 ff.

89 ¹ The second brick (not illustrated) measures 16 × 2¾ × 5 in. (41 × 7 × 12.7 cm.). A small, but clear photograph of it which shows detail better than the rubbing in our collections appears on pl. X of Thomas Torrance's "Burial Customs in Sz-chuan," *Journal of the North China Branch of the Royal Asiatic Society,* vol. 41 (1910), 57–75.

90 ¹ C. W. Bishop in "Long-Houses and Dragon-Boats," *Antiquity* (1938), pp. 411–424. O. Janse, *Archae-*

ological Research in Indo-China, p. 41, makes the interesting suggestion that certain types of Han houses built on top of double walls surrounding the compound were forerunners of the pile-supported dwelling. Janse has found such clay models in Han tombs in Indo-China. See his pls. 5, 45, 74, 87, 91, 98.

[2] A sketch of one bearing some resemblance to the construction shown in his rubbing can be seen in D. C. Graham's "Excavation of a Han Dynasty Tomb at Chungking," *Journal of the West China Border Research Society,* vol. 10 (1938), 185–190, fig. 11.

[3] Ségalen, text, fig. 102, 104, pls. XIV ff.

[4] A photograph of the original brick, unfortunately not very clear, appears in T. Torrance's "Notes on the Cave Tombs and Ancient Burial Mounds of Western Szechwan," *Journal of the West China Border Research Society,* vol. 4 (1930–1931), facing p. 88.

91 [1] *Hua yang kuo chih* (compiled in 347), chap. 3.

92 [1] Cf. Wallace Crawford, "The Salt Industry of Tzeliutsing," *China Journal of Science and Arts,* vol. 4 (1926), 169–175, 225–229, 281–290; vol. 5 (1926), 20–26.

[2] *T'ien kung k'ai wu,* ch. 5, by Sung Ying-hsing. Another informative account of the salt industry in Tzuliuching is the *Tzu liu ching chi* by Li Jung, published in 1890. This has been translated by Lien-che Tu Fang, "An Account of the Salt Industry at Tzu-liu-ching," *Isis,* vol. 39 (1948), 228–233. The accompanying illustrations are from the *Ssu ch'uan yen fa chih* of 1882 but are so nearly like those in the modern reprint of the *T'ien kung k'ai wu* that they must have come from an earlier edition of this seventeenth-century work. Cf. A. W. Hummel, *Eminent Chinese of the Ch'ing Period,* vol. 2, 691.

93 [1] The tower with the decorative bird perched on it bears some resemblance to those on the slab of unknown provenance shown in Chavannes, text, 1271. A good photograph of the original, now in the Boston Museum of Fine Arts, is given in Fischer, *Die chinesische Malerei der Han-Dynastie,* pl. 54. It may be worth noting that the terms *shih lou* and *shih men* both are names of constellations current in the Han period, the first being mentioned in *Shih chi,* ch. 27. But it seems improbable that there may be any astronomical symbolism in this prosaic scene.

94 [1] *Nan yang han hua hsiang chi,* no. 26, and *Nan yang han hua hsiang hui ts'un,* no. 3. No influence is implied, but there is an interesting and striking resemblance between this figure with human face, four limbs, and serpent's tail, frequently occurring in the Nan-yang reliefs, and the humanlike serpent in the fifteenth-century *Temptation* by Hugo von der Goes (H. Wölfflin, *Principles of Art History,* p. 181).

[2] An original rubbing of this brick occurs in *Ts'ui chen ko shu chuan chi,* vol. 1, fol. 8. The similarity, design, and size of this brick and no. 94 make them appear as if meant to be used in conjunction with one another.

95 [1] *Nan yang han hua hsiang hui ts'un,* no. 1. Another Nan-yang stone shows two birds with disk bodies (*Nan yang han hua hsiang chi,* no. 39). The three Nan-yang examples have bird heads; the three from Szechwan have human heads. Mirrors decorated with analogous birds are said to be of late Han date. Siren, *A History of Early Chinese Art,* vol. 2, p. 49, pl. 68A. Cf. Nils Palmgren, *Selected Chinese Antiquities,* p. 74, pl. 37:1.

[2] *Die chinesische Malerei der Han-Dynastie,* pl. 80, and p. 127. Similar paintings have been found in early fifth-century tombs in Manchuria. See Ikeuchi, *T'ung kou,* vol. 2, pl. 32. Further study may prove that the Szechwan bricks belong in the same general period. A detailed study of winged beings has been made by G. Ecke, "Atlantes and Caryatides in Chinese Architecture," *Bulletin of the Catholic University of Peking,* no. 7, but this type is not included.

96 [1] A line drawing of a similar scene, cast in bronze, has been found in a tomb at Lo-lang, Korea. The object which dates from the Han dynasty, or slightly later, clearly shows Hsi Wang Mu's throne to be composed of a dragon and a tiger. See Jung Keng, *Hai wai chi chin t'u lu,* vol. 3, no. 152. In this connection it is worth remembering that a lacquer tray, bearing an almost identical scene, made in Szechwan and dated A.D. 69 has been found in a Lo-lang tomb (see above, introduction).

97 [1] Chavannes, text, p. 19, n. 1 and p. 253, n. 1.

98 [1] Cf. D. C. Graham, "Ornamented Bricks and Tiles from Western Szechwan," *Journal of the West China Border Research Society,* vol. 10 (1938), 191 ff.

[2] *Shu chuan chi,* vol. 2, fol. 13.

99 [1] Laufer, *Chinese Grave Sculptures of the Han Period,* pl. IIb shows a stone slab from Shantung with relief of a man holding the sun symbol aloft, presumably protecting it from an attacking animal (eclipse?). What is probably the same brick is illustrated by Chavannes, text, no. 1243 and p. 268, but he interprets the scene as consisting of only one figure " ... un être bizarre dont la moitié inférieure est l'arrière-train d'un tigre ou d'un léopard vu de profil, tandis que la moitié supérieure est un buste d'homme qui est vu de face et qui tient dans ses deux mains élevées au-dessus de sa tête le disque du soleil."

[2] D. C. Graham, "Ornamented Bricks and Tiles from Western Szechwan," *Journal of the West China Border Research Society,* vol. 10 (1938), fig. 18. Our rubbing is from the topmost brick. See notes to no. 59.

GLOSSARY

ai   哀

Chang Heng   張衡

Chang Hsien-chung   張獻忠

Chao-hua   昭化

Chao Mai   趙買

Chengtu   成都

Ch'eng Wang   成王

Ch'eng Lien   成連

chi   戟

chia wu   甲午

Chialing   嘉陵江

Chiating   嘉定

Chien An   建安

ch'ien   乾

ch'in   琴

ch'in chuan   琴磚

Ch'in Shih Huang Ti   秦始皇帝

Ch'in Wu-yang   秦武陽

Ching K'o   荊軻

ch'ing lung   青龍

chiu-ch'ih-p'u   九尺鋪

Ch'iu Hu   秋胡

Ch'iung-lai   邛崍

Chou   周

Chou-t'sun   周村

chu ch'io (ch'iao)   朱雀

Chu Wei   朱鮪

ch'üeh   闕

Ch'un ch'iu   春秋

Chung Tzu-ch'i   鐘子期

Chungking   重慶

erh chu   栭柱

Fan Yü-ch'i   樊於期

feng   鳳

Feng Han-yi   馮漢驥

feng huang   鳳凰

fu   符

Romanization	Characters
Fu Hsi	伏羲
Fu Yi	傅毅
Honan	河南
Hou Yi	后羿
Hsi Ch'eng	希成
Hsi ching fu	西京賦
Hsi Wang Mu	西王母
Hsia Wu-chu	夏無且
hsiao	箭 山
Hsiao-t'ang Shan	孝堂
hsin mao	辛卯
Hsinchin	新津
Hsiu-ch'u	休屠
hsüan wu	玄武
Hsuchow	敘州
Hua-p'ai-fang	花牌坊
huang	凰
I-pin	宜賓
Kansu	甘肅
K'ai-feng	開封
K'ai Mu ch'üeh	開母闕
Kao Yi ch'üeh	高頤闕 文
ku ch'üan wen	古泉文
Kuang Han	廣漢磚
k'uang chuan	壙磚
kuei	圭

Romanization	Characters
k'ung chuan	空瀨 磚記
Lai hsiang chi	鄉虎洞
lao hu tung	老虎善尤
Li Shan	李陽博
Li Yu	李尤
Liao-yang	遼陽
liu po	六博
Lu	魯 西康
Lu Shan, Sikang	蘆山子洞
man tzu tung	蠻子江
Meng Tzu	孟子
Min	岷江
Ming	明 魚山
Mu-yü Shan	木魚
Nan-ch'ang	南常京
Nanking	南京
Nan-yang	南陽號
nien hao	年號
Nü Kua	女媧
pai hu	白虎 文山
p'an ch'ih wen	蟠螭子縣山
Pao-tzu Shan	寶子縣
P'eng Hsien	彭縣
P'eng Shan	彭山
pi	璧
Pien-liang	汴梁

46

Po Ya 伯牙

Po Yü 柏榆

Shantung 山東

Shao Shih ch'üeh 少室闕

Shen ch'üeh 沈闕

shih 拾

Shih ching 詩經

shih lou 市樓

Shu 蜀

Sikang 西康

Szechwan 四川

T'ai Shih ch'üeh 太室闕

t'ao t'ieh 饕餮

Teng-feng hsien 登封縣

t'i p'ing 踢瓶

t'iao 條

Tien Mu 電母

Ting chia yao tien 丁家腰店

t'ing chang 亭長

t'ing chang chuan 亭長磚

Tuan Fang 端方

tung shih men 東市門

tzu ch'üeh 子闕

Tzu-liu-ching 自流井

Wang Chih-tzu 王稚子

Wang Hui, Po-chao 王暉伯昭

wei ting 未定

Wen Yu 聞宵

Wu Chin-ting 吳金鼎

Wu fu 舞賦

wu kan 舞竿

Wu Liang 武梁

Wu Liang Tz'u 武梁祠

Ya-an hsien 雅安縣

Yang Chih-kao 楊枝高

Yi ching 易經

Yi-wen 義文

Yuan-kung 元公

Yün-kang 雲岡

Yung P'ing 永平

Yung Yuan 永元

BIBLIOGRAPHY

ANDERSSON, J. G., "Hunting Magic in the Animal Style," *Bulletin of the Museum of Far Eastern Antiquities*, no. 4 (1932), 221–317.

Baber, E., *Travels and Researches in the Interior of China*, London, 1886.

Bachhofer, Ludwig, *A Short History of Chinese Art*, New York, 1946.

Bishop, W. C., "Long-Houses and Dragon-Boats," *Antiquity* (1938), 411–424.

———, "The Problem of the Min River Caves," *Chinese Social and Political Science Review*, vol. 10 (1926), 46–61.

Bodde, Derk, *Statesman, Patriot, and General in Ancient China*, New Haven, 1940.

Bückens, F., "Les Antiquités funéraires du Honan Central," *Bulletin de la Société d'Anthropologie de Bruxelles*, vol. 36 (1921), 59–164.

Cammann, Schuyler, "Tibetan Monster Masks," *Journal of the West China Border Research Society*, ser. A, 12 (1940), 11–16.

Chavannes, Edouard, *Mission archéologique dans la Chine septentrionale*. I, 1, *La Sculpture à l'époque des Han*, Paris, 1913 (*Publications de l'École Française d'Extrême-Orient*, xiii, 1).

Crawford, Wallace, "The Salt Industry of Tze-liutsing," *China Journal of Science and Arts*, vol. 4 (1926), 169–175, 225–229, 281–290; 5 (1926), 20–26.

Detroit Institute of Arts, *Exhibition of Ancient Chinese Ritual Bronzes Loaned by C. T. Loo & Co.*, 1940.

Drake, F. S., "Sculptured Stones of the Han Dynasty," *Monumenta Serica*, vol. 8 (1943), 280–318.

Eberhard, A., and W., *Die Mode der Han und Chin Zeit*, Antwerp, 1946.

Eder, Matthias, "Eiserne Degen und Schwerter aus der Han-Zeit," *Monumenta Serica*, vol. 8 1943), 394–400.

Edgerton, W. F., "Two Notes on the Flying Gallop," *Journal of the American Oriental Society*, vol. 56 (1936), 178–188.

Fairbank, Wilma, "The Offering Shrines of 'Wu Liang Tz'u,'" *Harvard Journal of Asiatic Studies*, vol. 6 (1941), 1–36.

———, "A Structural Key to Han Mural Art," *Harvard Journal of Asiatic Studies*, vol. 7 (1942), 52–58.

Fischer, Otto, *Die chinesische Malerei der Han-Dynastie*, Berlin, 1931.

Franke, W., "Die Han-Zeitlichen Felsengraeber bei Chia-ting," *Studia Serica*, vol. 7 (1948), 19–39.

Graham, D. C., "The Ancient Caves of Szechwan Province," *Proceedings of the United States Museum*, vol. 80 (1932), art. 16.

———, "Excavation of a Han Dynasty Tomb at Chungking," *Journal of the West China Border Research Society*, vol. 10 (1938), 185–190.

———, "Ornamented Bricks and Tiles from Western Szechwan," *Journal of the West China Border Research Society*, vol. 10 (1938), 191 ff.

———, "Persistence of Custom as Illustrated in

the Collection of Han Dynasty Clay Images in the West China Museum," *Journal of the West China Border Research Society,* vol. 6 (1934).

Hentze, Carl, *Chinese Tomb Figures, A Study in the Beliefs and Folklore of Ancient China,* London, 1928.

———, *Die Sakralbronzen und ihre Bedeutung in den fruehchinesischen Kulturen,* Antwerp, 1941. 2 vols.

———, *Objets rituels, croyances et dieux de la Chine et de l'Amérique,* Anvers, 1936.

Hummel, A. E., *Eminent Chinese of the Ch'ing Period,* Washington, 1943–1944. 2 vols.

Janse, Olov R. T., *Archaeological Research in Indo-China,* vol. 1 (Cambridge, 1947). (Harvard-Yenching Institute Monograph Series, 7.)

———, *Briques et objets céramiques funéraires le l'époque des Han, appartenant à C. T. Loo et Cie.,* Paris, 1936.

———, "Notes sur quelques épées anciennes trouvées en Chine," *Bulletin of the Museum of Far Eastern Antiquities,* vol. 2 (1930), 67–134.

Kaplan, S., "On the Origin of the TLV Mirror," *Revue des arts asiatiques,* vol. 11 (1937), 21–24.

Karlbeck, Orvar, *Catalogue of the Collection of Chinese and Korean Bronzes at Hallwyl House, Stockholm,* Stockholm, 1938.

Karlgren, Bernhard, "Legends and Cults in Ancient China," *Museum of Far Eastern Antiquities,* no. 18 (1946), 199–365.

Laufer, B., *Chinese Grave Sculptures of the Han Period,* New York, London, Paris, 1911.

———, *Chinese Clay Figures, Part I, Prolegomena on the History of Defensive Armor,* 1914. (Field Museum of Natural History Anthropological Series, 13, no. 2).

———, "Chinese Sarcophagi," *Oestasiatische Zeitschrift,* vol. 1 (1912–1913), 318–334.

Legge, James, *The Chinese Classics,* vol. 2: *The Works of Mencius,* 2d ed., Oxford, 1895. Vol. 4: *The She King, or The Book of Poetry,* London, 1871.

Li, Jung, "An Account of the Salt Industry at Tzu-liu-ching," *Isis,* vol. 39 (1948), 228–233.

Lodge, J. E., A. G. Wenley, and J. A. Pope, *A Descriptive and Illustrative Catalog of Chinese Bronzes,* Washington, 1946.

Lopez, R. S., "Silk Industry in the Byzantine Empire," *Speculum,* vol. 20 (1945) 1–42.

Maenchen-Helfen, Otto, "Der Schuss auf die Sonen," *Wiener Zeitschrift für die Kunde des Morgenlandes,* vol. 44 (1936), 75–95.

———, "From China to Palmyra," *Art Bulletin,* vol. 25 (1943), 358–362.

Maspero, Henri, "La vie privée en Chine a l'époque des Han," *Revue des arts asiatiques,* vol. 7 (1932), 185–201.

Petrie, Sir Flinders, *Decorative Patterns of the Ancient World,* London, 1930.

Rudolph, R. C., "Han Tomb Reliefs from Szechwan," *Archives of the Chinese Art Society of America,* vol. 4 (1950).

Salmony, A., "Le Mascaron et l'anneau dans l'art sur les pendentifs et les appliqués," *Revue des arts asiatiques,* vol. 8 (1934), 182–186.

Ségalen, Victor, Gilbert de Voisins, and Jean Lartigue, *Mission archéologique en Chine,* Paris, 1923–1924. 1 vol., 2 portfolios.

Ségalen, Victor, "Premier exposé des résultats archéologiques obtenus dans la Chine occidental," *Journal Asiatique,* vol. 6 (1915), ser. 11, 281–306.

Simmons, Pauline, *Chinese Patterned Silks,* New York, 1948.

Siren, Osvald, *A History of Early Chinese Painting,* vol. 1, London, 1933.

Soper, A. C., "Early Chinese Landscape Painting," *Art Bulletin,* vol. 23 (1941), 141–164.

Stein, Sir Aurel, *Innermost Asia,* Oxford, 1928. 3 vols.

Tomita, Kojiro, *Portfolio of Chinese Paintings in the Museum,* 2d ed., Cambridge, 1938.

Torii, Ryuzo, *Sculptured Stone Tombs of the Liao Dynasty,* Peking, 1942.

Torrance, Thomas, "Burial Customs in Sz-chuan," *Journal of the North China Branch of the Royal Asiatic Society,* vol. 41 (1910), 57–75.

———, "Notes on the Cave Tombs and Ancient Burial Mounds of Western Szechwan," *Journal of the West China Border Research Society*, vol. 4 (1930–1931), 88–96.

Trever, Camilla, *Excavations in Northern Mongolia*, Leningrad, 1932 (Memoirs of the Academy of History of Material Culture, III).

Waley, Arthur, *An Introduction to the Study of Chinese Painting*, London, 1923.

————, *The Temple and Other Poems*, London, 1923.

White, W. C., *Tomb Tile Pictures of Ancient China*, Toronto, 1939.

White, W. C., and P. M. Millman, "An Ancient Chinese Sun-dial," *Journal of the Royal Astronomical Society of Canada* (November, 1938), 417–430.

Wölfflin, Heinrich, *Principles of Art History*, New York, 1932.

Yang, Lien-sheng, "A Note on the So-called TLV Mirrors and the Game of Liu-po," *Harvard Journal of Asiatic Studies*, vol. 9 (1945–1947), 202–206.

Yetts, W. P., *The Cull Chinese Bronzes*, London, 1939.

————, "Discoveries of the Koslov Expedition," reprint from *Burlington Magazine*, April, 1926.

————, "The Horse: A Factor in Early Chinese History," *Eurasia Septentrionalis Antiqua*, vol. 9 (1934), 1–55.

————, "Notes on Chinese Roof-Tiles," *Transactions of the Oriental Ceramic Society*, vol. 7 (1927–1928), 13–42.

CHINESE WORKS

IN ACCORDANCE with Chinese usage, works are quoted by title rather than by author and are generally referred to in this manner in the footnotes. Articles in journals and anthologies are listed by author. When Western translations of titles are given this indicates that the work has this subtitle.

Chao Pang-yen, "Han hua so chien yu hsi k'ao," *Ch'ing chu ts'ai yüan p'ei hsien sheng liu shih wu sui lun wen chi (Studies Presented to Ts'ai Yüan-p'ei on his Sixty-fifth Birthday)*, vol. 1 (Peiping, 1933), 525–538.

Ch'ien p'i t'ing ku chuan lu, by Lu Hsin-yüan. 1891.

Chin shih so, by Feng Yün-p'eng and Feng Yün-yüan. 1821.

Chin shih wen tzu pien yi, by Hsing Chu. 1810.

Chuan men ming chia, another name for *Kuang ts'ang chuan lu.*

Chung kuo hui hua shih, by Yü Chien-hua. Shanghai, 1936. 2 vols.

趙邦彥　　漢畫所見游戲考　　慶祝蔡元培先生六十五歲論文集

千甓亭古專錄　　　　陸心源

金石索　　馮雲鵬　　馮雲鵷

金石文字辨異　　　　邢澍

專門名家

中國繪畫史　　　俞劍華

Chung kuo ming ch'i (*A Brief History of Chinese Mortuary Objects*), by Cheng Te-k'un and Shen Wei-chün. Peiping, 1933. (Yenching Journal of Chinese Studies, Monograph Series No. 1.)

Hai wai chi chin t'u lu, by Jung Keng. Peiping, 1935.

Han pei lu wen, by Ma Pang-yü. 1918.

Han tai k'uang chuan chi lu, by Wang chen-to. Peiping, 1935.

Han wei liu ch'ao chuan wen, by Wang Shu-nan. Shanghai, 1935.

Han wu liang tz'u hua hsiang lu, by Jung Keng. Peiping, 1936.

Heng nung chung mu yi wen, by Lo Chen-yü. 1918.

Jen Nai-ch'iang, "Lu shan hsin ch'u han shih t'u k'ao," "Pien wang hui shih kuan fou tiao," *K'ang tao yüeh k'an,* 4:6, 7; 5:1 (1942–1943).

Ku lieh nü chuan, by Liu Hsiang (29–8 B.C.). (*Ssu pu ts'ung k'an,* ed.)

Kuang ts'ang chuan lu, by Tsou An. 1917.

Li shih, by Hung Kua, *Ssu pu ts'ung k'an,* ed.

Liao yang pei yüan hua pi ku mu chi lueh (A Brief Study of the Tombs with Frescoes Discovered in Liao-yang, Liang-ning Province), by Li Wen-hsin. *Bulletin No. 1 of the Preparatory Committee, National Museum of Shen Yang,* 1947.

中國明器

　　　鄭德坤　　沈維鈞

海外吉金圖錄　　　　容庚

漢碑錄文　　馬邦玉

漢代壙磚集錄　　　王振鐸

漢魏六朝磚文　　　王樹枏

漢武梁祠畫象錄　　　容庚

恒農冢墓遺文　　　羅振玉

任乃強　　蘆山新出漢石圖考　　　　辨王暉石棺浮雕

　　　　　　康導月刊

古列女傳　　劉向　　　　　　四部叢刊

廣倉磚錄　　　鄒安

隸釋　洪适　　四部叢刊

遼陽北園畫壁古墓記略

　　　　　　　　　　李文信

Liu Fu, "Hsi han tai shih tai ti jih kuei," *Kuo hsüeh chi k'an*, vol. 3, no. 4 (1932), 573–610.

Mu t'ao hsüan ku chuan t'u lu, by Wu T'ing-k'ang. 1851.

Nan yang han hua hsiang chi, by Kuan Po-yi. Shanghai, 1930.

Nan yang han hua hsiang hui ts'un, by Sun Wen-ch'ing. Nanking, 1936.

Shang, Ch'eng-tso, "Erh chu," *Chung kuo wen hua yen chiu hui k'an*, vol. 1 (1941), 41–60.

————, "Ssu-chuan hsin chin teng ti han yai mu chuan mu k'ao lüeh," *Chin ling hsüeh pao*, vol. 10 (1940), 1–18.

Shang chou yi ch'i t'ung k'ao (*The Bronzes of Shang and Chou*), by Jung Keng. Peiping, 1941. 2 vols. (Yenching Journal of Chinese Studies, Monograph Series no. 17.)

Szu ch'uan ku tai wen hua shih (*A History of Ancient Szechwan*), by Cheng Te-k'un. Chengtu, 1946. (West China Union University Museum, Monograph Series No. 1.)

T'ai p'ing yü lan, compiled by Li Fang (983). 1807 ed.

T'ien kung k'ai wu, by Sung Ying-hsing (1637). 1927 ed.

Ts'ui chen ko shu chuan chi, compiled by Tseng Min-yu. Chengtu, 1948.

T'un an ku chuan ts'un, by Wu Yin. 1910.

劉復　西漢時代的日晷　　　　　國立北京大學國學季刊

慕陶軒古磚圖錄　　　　　吳廷康

南陽漢畫象集　　　　　關百益

南陽漢畫象彙存　　　　　　孫文青

商承祚　　　　柟柱　　中國文化研究會刊

　　　　四川新津等地漢崖墓專墓考略　　　　　金陵學報

適周彝器通考　　　　　　　　　容庚

四川古代文化史　　　　　　　鄭德坤

太平御覽　　　　　李昉

天工開物　　　　宋應星

萃珍閣蜀專集　　　　　曾敏祐

邀盦古專存　　　吳隱

Tung ching meng hua lu, by Meng Yüan-lao (1147) (*Hsüeh chin t'ao yüan,* ed.).

Tzu liu ching chi, by Li Jung. 1890.

Wu liang tz'u t'ang hua hsiang k'ao, by Ch'ü Chung-jung. 1926.

東京夢華錄　　　孟元老　　　　學津討原

自流井記　　李榕

武梁祠堂畫象考　　　　瞿中溶

JAPANESE WORKS

CHŌSEN KOSEKI KENKYŪ KWAI, *Rakurō saikyō tsuka* (*The Tomb of Painted Basket of Lo-lang*). Seoul, 1934 (Reports of Archaeological Research, Vol. 1, Society for the Investigation of Korean Antiquities), English summary.

Hamada Kosaku, *Shina ko minki deishō zusetsu*, 2d ed., Tōkyō, 1927. 2 vols.

————, "Kandai no kaiga ni tsuite," Mori Osamu, *Ying ch'eng tzu*, pp. 39–44.

————, *Tōa kōkogaku kenkyū*. Tōkyō, 1943.

Harada Yoshito, *Lo-lang* (*A report on the Excavation of Wang Hsü's Tomb in the Lo-lang Province, an Ancient Chinese Colony in Korea*). Tōkyō, 1933. English summary.

————, *Kan rikuchō no fukushoku* (*Chinese Dress and Personal Ornaments in the Han and Six Dynasties*), Tōkyō, 1937 (Tōyō Bunko Ronsō, Series A, Vol. XXIII.) English summary.

————, *Shina koki zukō*, pt. 2. Tōkyō, 1937.

朝鮮古蹟研究會　樂浪彩篋冢

濱田耕作　支那古明器泥象圖説

　　漢代の繪畫に就いて　森修　營城子

　　東亜考古學研究

原田淑人　樂浪

　　漢六朝の服飾

　　支那古器圖考

Heibonsha, *Sekai bijutsu zenshū*, vol. 3. Tōkyō, 1928.

Ikeuchi Hiroshi, Umehara Sueji, and Harada Yoshito, *T'ung Kou*, Tōkyō, 1938. 2 vols. English summary.

Mizuno Seiichi, *Unkō sekibutsu gun*. Ōsaka, 1943.

Mori Osamu, Naitō Hiroshi, *Ying-ch'eng tzu*. (*Report upon the Excavation of the Han Brick-tomb with Fresco-paintings.*) Tōkyō and Kyōto, 1934 (Archaeologia Orientalis, vol. 4). English summary.

Sekino Tei, *Shina santōshō ni okeru kandai fumbo no hyōshoku*. Tōkyō, 1916.

Umehara Sueji, *Kan izen no kokyō no kenkyū* (*L'Étude sur le miroir anterieur à la dynastie des Han*). Kyōto, 1935. French summary.

————, *Shina kandai kinenmei shikki zusetsu*. Kyōto, 1943.

Yagi Jōzaburō, *Manshū kōkogaku*. Tōkyō, 1944.

————, *Ryōyō hakken no hekiga koseki* (Tōyō Gakuhō, vol. 11, pt. 1).

平凡社　世界美術全集

池内　宏　　　　梅原末治　　　濱田　通溝

水野清一　　雲岡石佛群

森修　内藤寬　營城子

關野貞　支那山東省に於ける漢代墳墓の表飾

梅原末治　　漢以前の古鏡の研究

　　　支那漢代紀年銘漆器圖説

八木獎三郎　滿洲考古學

　　　遼陽發見の壁畫古墳

INDEX

Numbers in italics refer to pages of the Introduction. Other numbers refer to the rubbings and their descriptions.

Archaeology, Chinese, *3 ff.*
Archer, 28, 55, 76, 85
Architecture, 26, 27, 86, 87, 90
Attendants, 54, 87, 88, 96

Balls, 78
Basket, 9, 37
Beam ends, 30–31, 32, 33
Bird, three-legged, 96, 97, 99
Birds, 28, 30–31, 48, 49, 54–56, 60–63, 67, 98
Bow, 76, 85, 89; reflex, 89
Buckets, 91, 92

Cap, quilted, 37
Carp, 22
Cart, 2, 84, 90; covered, 5, 83
Cassia tree, 58, 94
Cave tombs, *6–17*
Chariots, 39, 52, 53, 82, 88, 89, 150
Chi (weapon), 68
Ch'in (lute), 56, 77
Ch'in Shih Huang Ti, 13, 15
Ch'in Wu-yang, 16
Chu Wei reliefs, 45
Ch'üeh (monument), *6, 7,* 27, 50, 51, 52, 86–89
Ching K'o, 13, 15

Chi'u Hu, 37
Coffins, 7, *8*
Coin design, 28, 66, 98
Coins, *8, 17*
Costume, 37, 64, 65, 68, 77–80
Cross: formée, 32; maltese, 32
Crossbow, 6, 91

Dagger, 70
Dais, 14, 41. *See also* Throne
Dancer, 30–31, 77, 78, 81
Dancing, 30–31, 77, 78
Dark Warrior. *See* North, symbol for
Dates, *19,* 46, 75, 98
Deer, 54
Derrick, 91, 92
Design, pattern, 32, 36, 87, 98, 99, 100. *See also* Coin design, *T'ao t'ieh.*
Dog, 20, 34
Doors, tomb 60–71
Dragon, 29, 54, 73; spined, 47, 73; winged, 56, 69
Drug of immortality, 96, 97, 100
Drum, 77, 78, 81; tower, 93
Dwarf, 1

East, symbol for, 29, 73
Erh chu (bracket), 28, 35, 90

Fan Yü-Ch'i, 16
Feathers, 38
Feng huang, 48, 86
Festive scenes, 77, 78, 79
Filial piety, *3,* 25
Fireplaces, 7
Fish, 12, 21, 22, 76
Fisherman, 11
Fishing pole, 10
Flying gallop, 39
Fox, nine-tailed, 96, 97, 100
Fu Hsi, 58, 59, 99

Games, 56, 57, 80
Gaming board, 56, 57, 80
Gas, natural, 91
Geese, 76
Grave goods, *17–18*
Green Dragon. *See* East, symbol for
Guardian, 7, 8, 68, 70, 87

Han dynasty: bricks, *18–19*; bronzes, *4, 17*; coins, *8, 17*; lacquer, *4*; literature, *3*; murals, *4, 5*; painting, *3–4*; pottery, *4, 17*; reliefs, *3–6, 8, 17*; textiles, *4*; tombs, *4, 6–19*
Hare, lunar, 58, 96, 97, 100
Harness, 83; tandem, 84
Harvest, 76
Horror vacui, 17
Horse, winged, 46
Horses, 17, 18, 30–31, 39, 51, 82–85, 88, 89
Hou Yi, 55
House, 25, 26, 90
Hsi Wang Mu, *4, 19*, 96, 97, 100
Hsia Wu-chü, 13
Hsiao (dancing staff), 42
Hunters, 76, 91, 92
Hunting, 76, 91, 92

Inscriptions, *19*, 46, 64, 65, 70, 75, 93, 98

Jugglers, 78

Ku ch'üan wen, 28. *See* Coin design.
Kuei (tablet), 37

Lacquer. *See* Han dynasty, Szechwan
Ladder, 90
Lance, 51
Liaoyang, *4*
Liu po (game), 56, 57, 80
Lo-lang, *4*
Lute, 56, 77

Man tzu tung (caves), *6*
Market, 93
Mask, 34, 38, 40; and ring, 60–63, 67–71; animal, 7, 8; feline, 10
Mastiff, 20
Mats, 77–79
Monster mask, 33, 60–63, 67–71
Moon, symbol for, 29, 58, 59, 94, 96, 97, 99
Musical instruments, 56, 77. *See also* Drum.
Mythological beings, 4, 54, 56–59, 75, 96–100

North, symbol for, 29, 74, 99
Nü Kua, 58, 59, 99

Oven, 91, 92
Ox, 90

Parasol, 38, 82
Peacock, 30–31, 55
Perspective, 91, 92
Pi (disk), 47
Pipes, 91, 92
Po Ya, 56
Po Yu, 3
Porte-épée, 68
Portrait, 44, 45, 65
Pulley, 91, 92

Quiver, 43, 85

Ram, 23
Red Bird. *See* South, symbol for
Reliefs: Chiating, *6, 8, 17*; Hsinchin, *8, 17*; comparison of, *8, 17*; content of, *19*; Shantung, *3–4, 17*; Szechwan, *6, 17*
Roof: construction, 26; tiled, 25, 81, 86, 87, 90, 93
Rope, 18, 20, 26
Rubbings, *17*

Salt: mining, 91, 92; well, 91, 92
Sarcophagi, *7, 8*, 72–75
Scabbard, 68
Scythes, 76
Servant, 9, 66
Shark, 21
Shantung reliefs, *3–4, 17*
Sheep, 23
Shepherd's crook, 10
Shield, 40, 43
Snake, 8, 28
South, symbol for, 24, 49, 99
Stars, 94
Stone boxes, *7, 8*
Stove, *7*, 93
Sun, symbol for, 58, 59, 96, 97, 99
Sundial, 32
Sword, 37, 40, 43, 68, 70, 81; iron, *17*, 68
Symbol of authority, 42
Szechwan: lacquer, *4*; neolithic finds, *5*; paleolithic finds, *5*; Province, *5*; reliefs, *6*, 17

Tables, 56, 77, 79
T'ao t'ieh, 33. *See* Monster mask.
Throne, 96, 97, 100
Tiger, 19, 28, 71, 72
Tile ends, 30–31, 32, 33, 66
Tiles, types of, *18–19*
T'ing chang (guardian), 68, 70, 87
Toad, lunar, 29, 94, 99
Tomb: dates, *19*; doors, *7, 8,* 60–64, 66–71; figurines, *18, 9,* 20; shafts, *7, 8*; tiles, *18–19*
Tongue-and-groove, 90, 99
Tortoise, 99
Tortoise and snake, 29, 74
Tree, 37, 48, 54

Vessels, food, 57, 77–79
Vestibules, loggia, *6–7, 17*

Wang Hsü, tomb of, *4*
Water lilies, 76
Weapons, 8, 17, 37, 40, 43, 51, 68, 70, 81. *See also* Bow.
West, symbol for, 28, 72
Wheels, 89; solid, 2
White Tiger. *See* West, symbol for
Wings, 19, 54, 71
Wu Liang reliefs, *3–4 et seq.*
Wu shrines, *3–4*

Ying-ch'eng-tzu, *4*

PART II

Plates

RELIEFS ON STONE

CHIATING

I

2

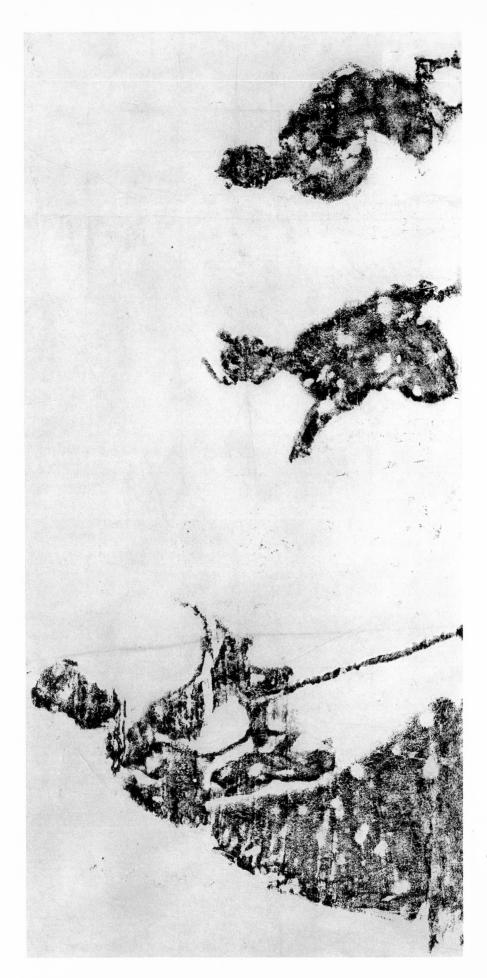

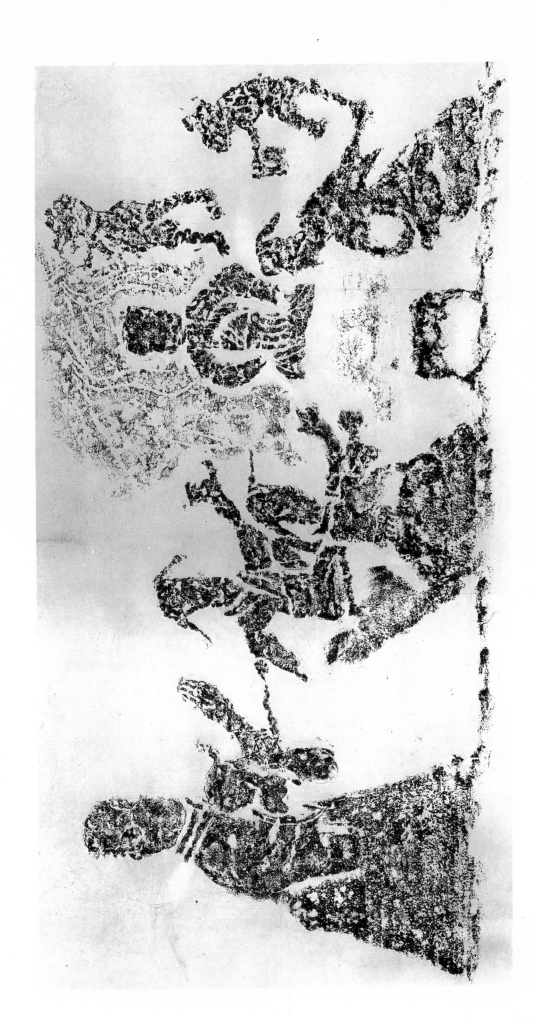

4

5

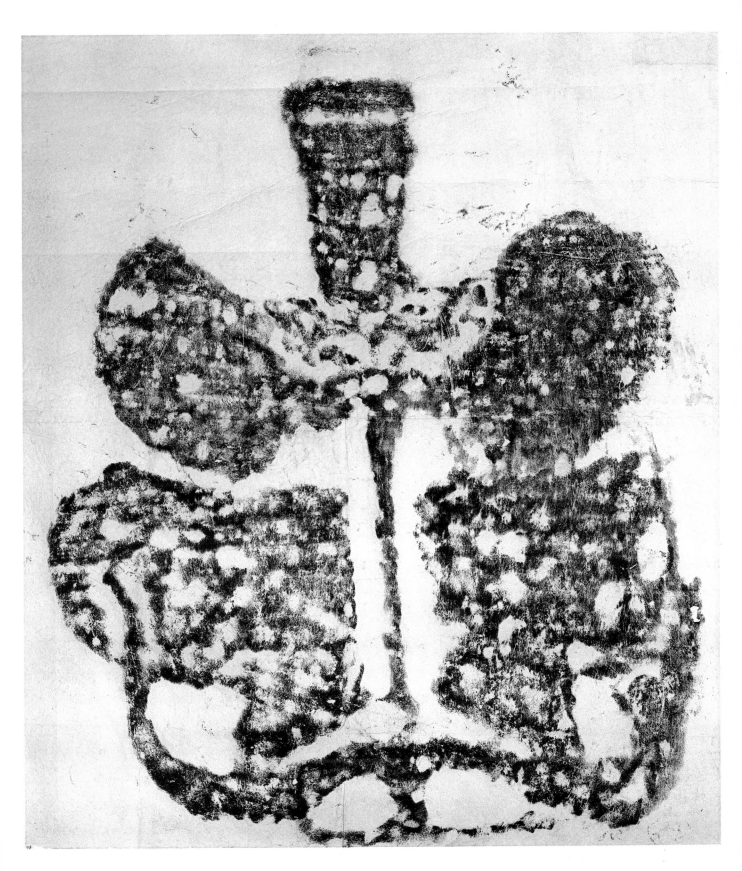

6

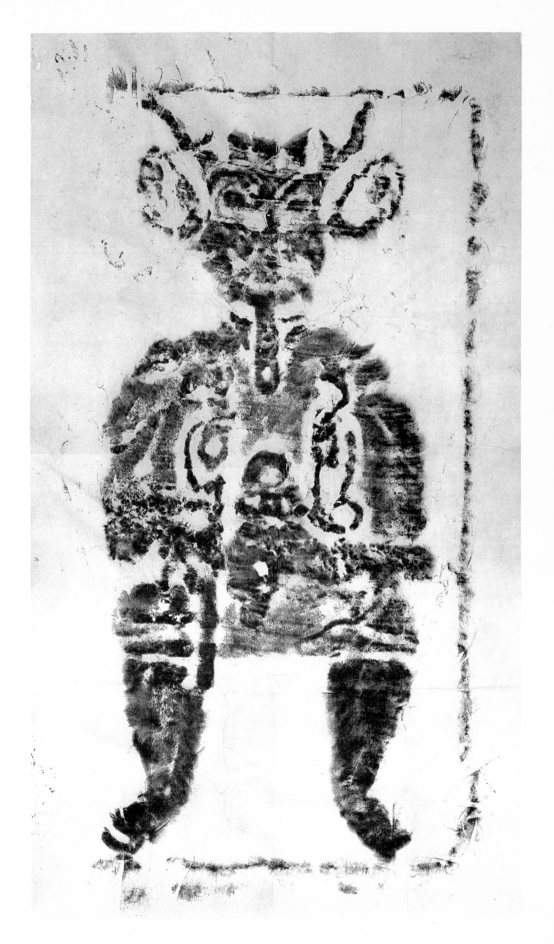

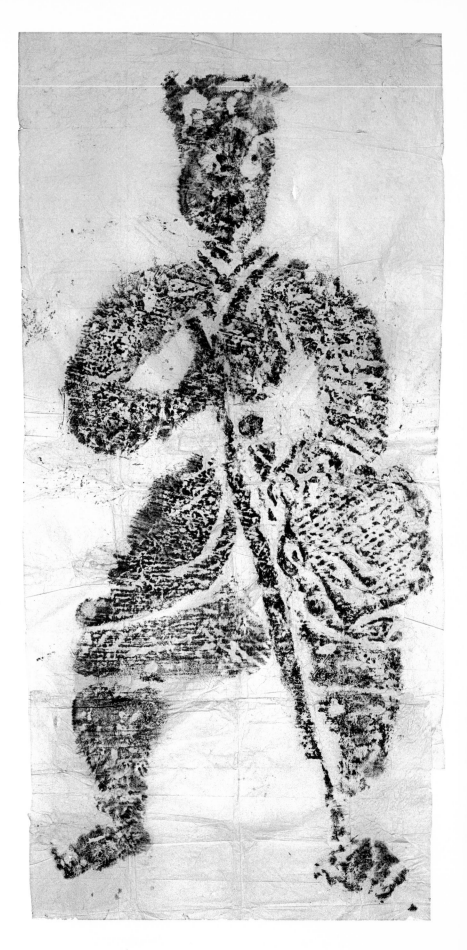

9

II

12

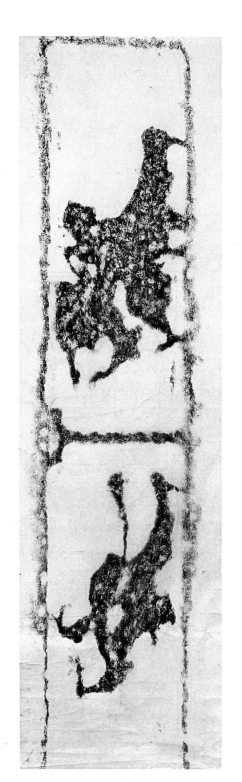

13

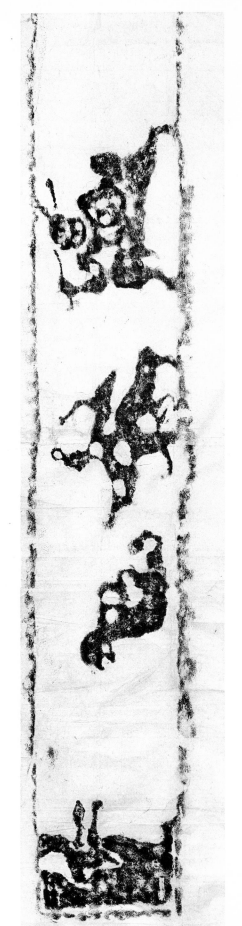

14

15

91

17

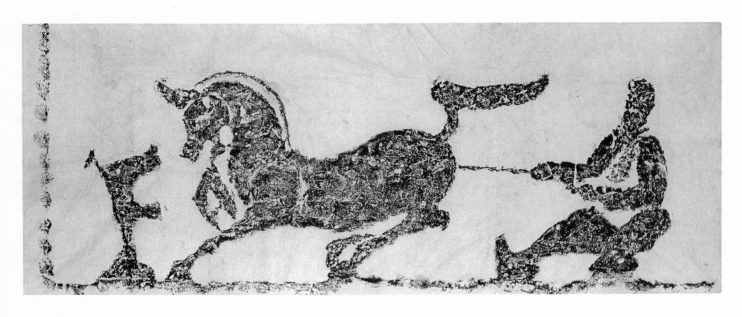

18

19

20

21

22

23

24

25

26

27

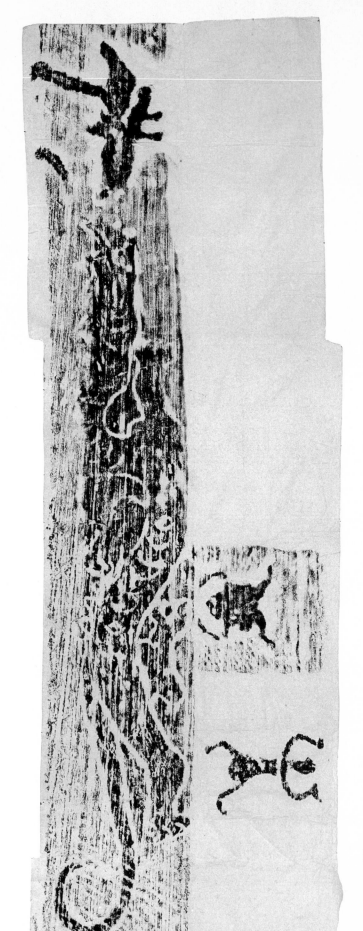

28

29

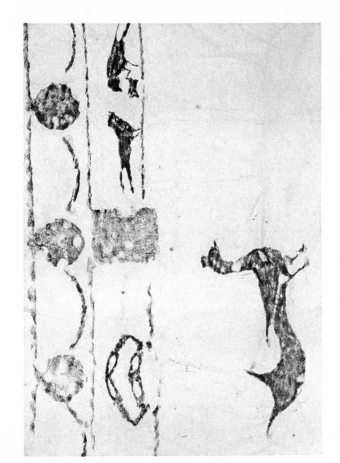

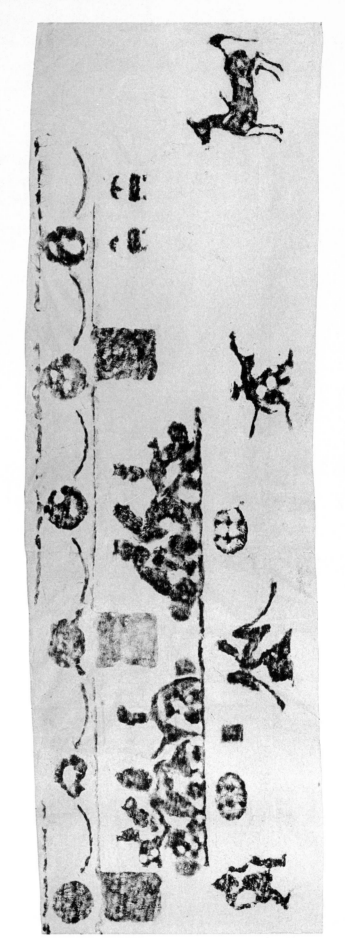

32

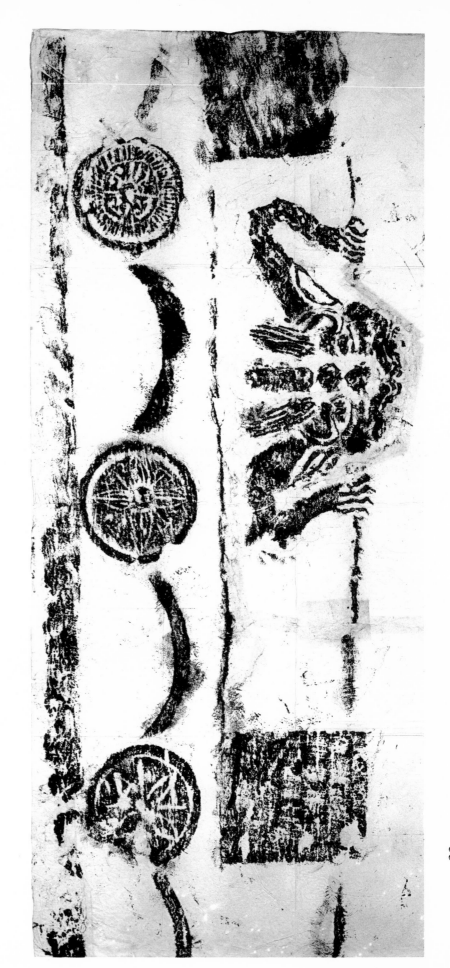

33

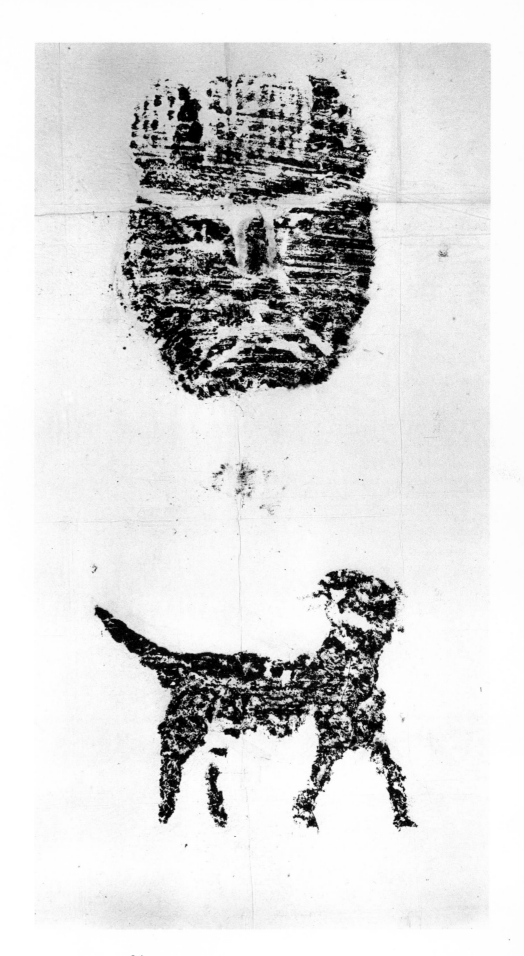

34

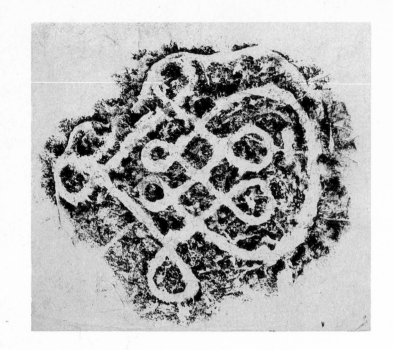

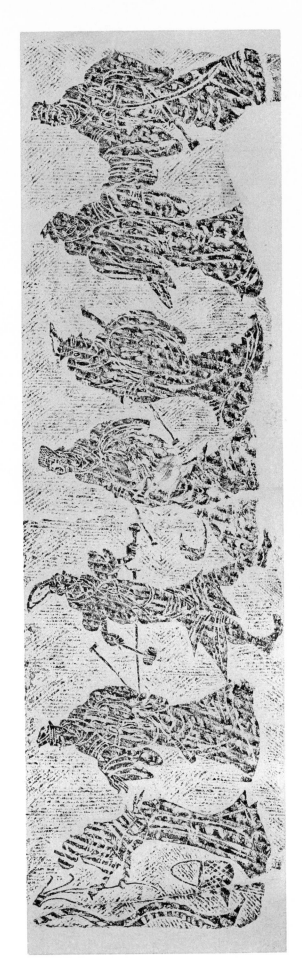

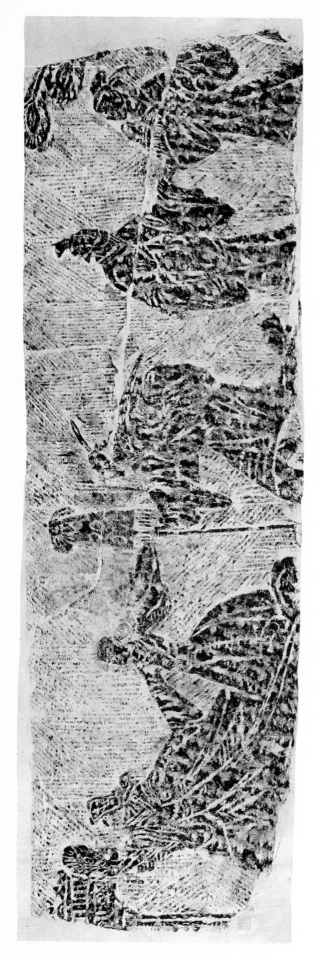

38

39

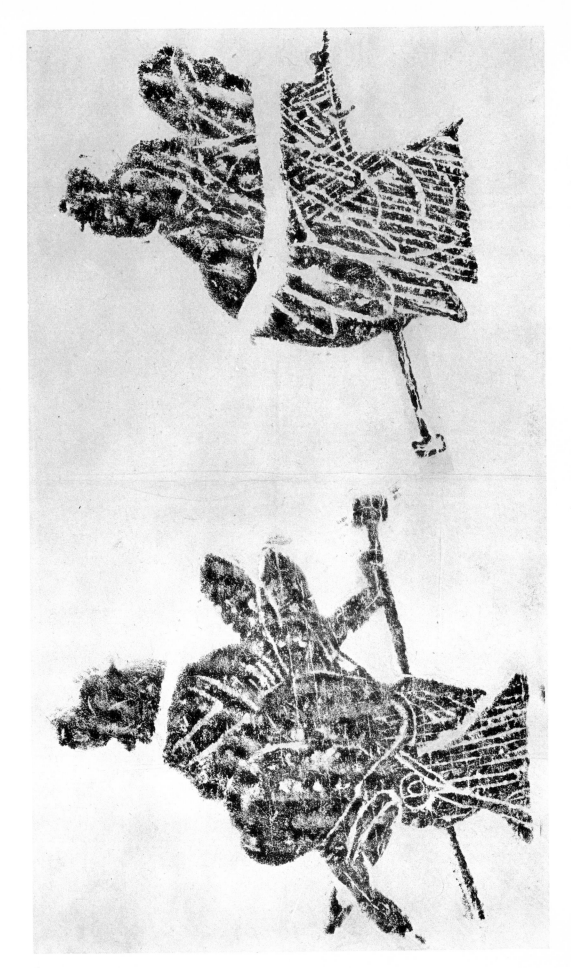

43

44

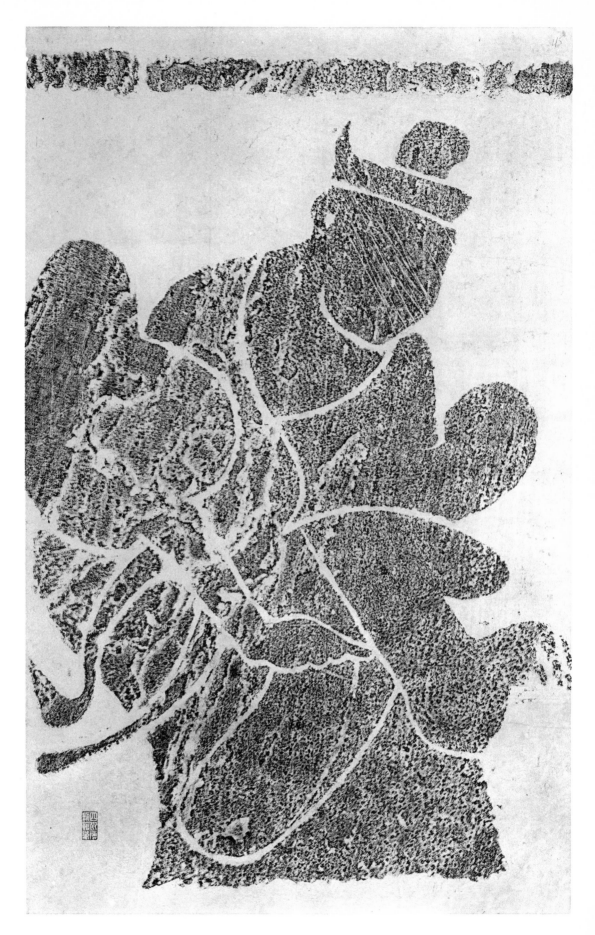

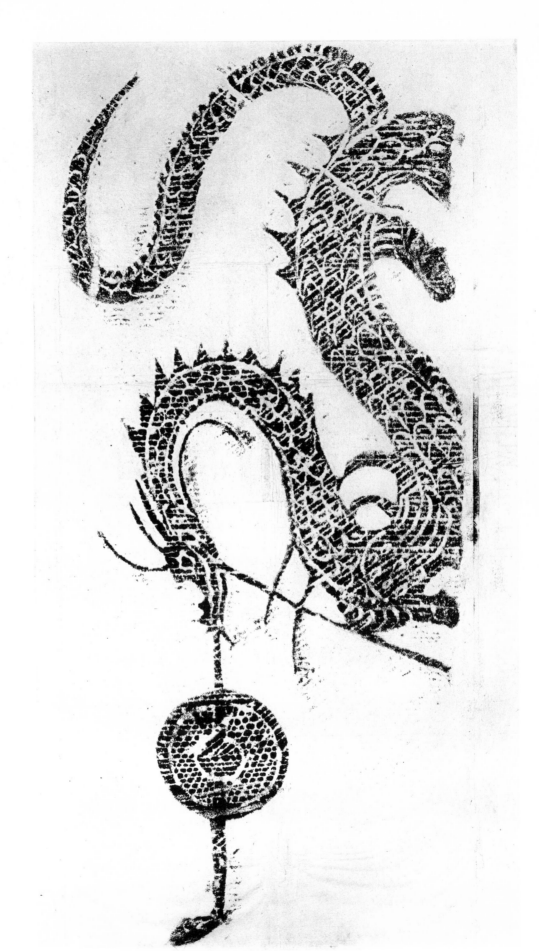

48

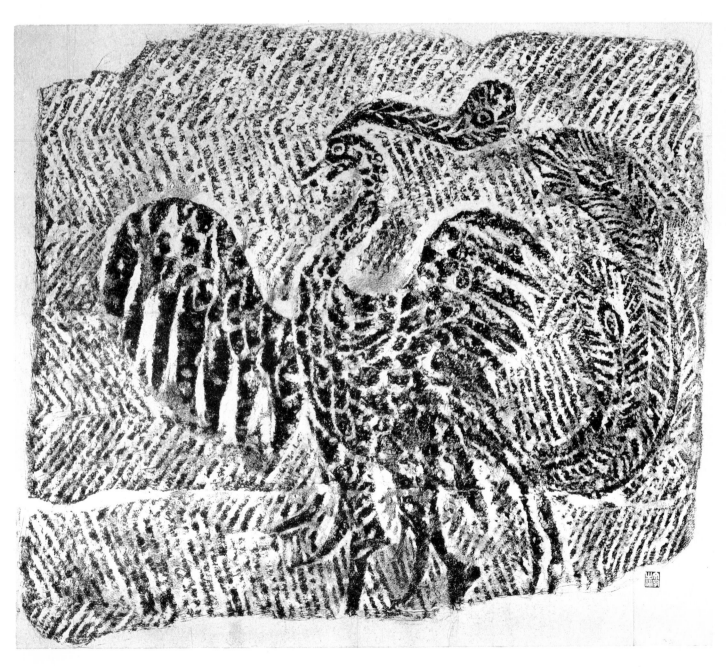

49

50

51

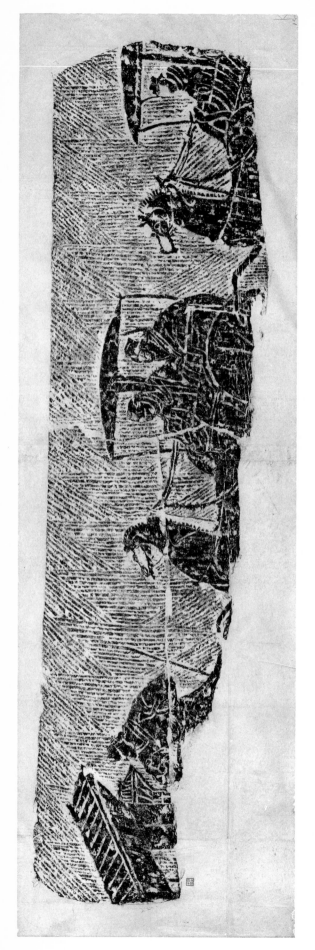

52

53

54

55

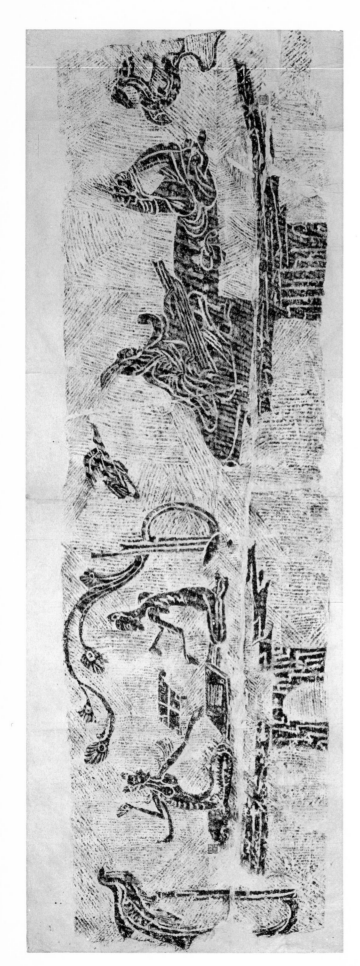

56

57

58

59

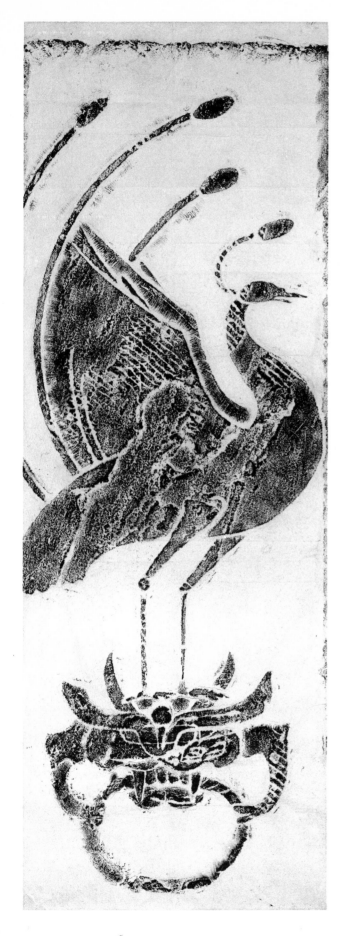

60   61

62

63

66

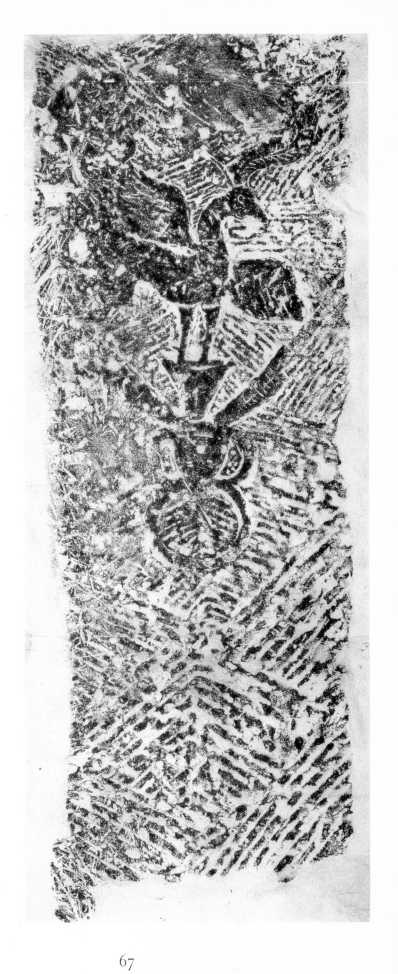

CHENGTU AND

LU SHAN

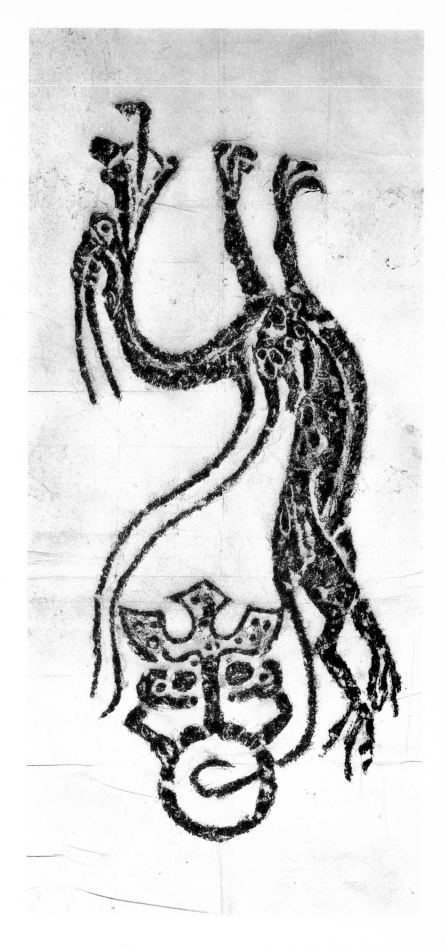

70

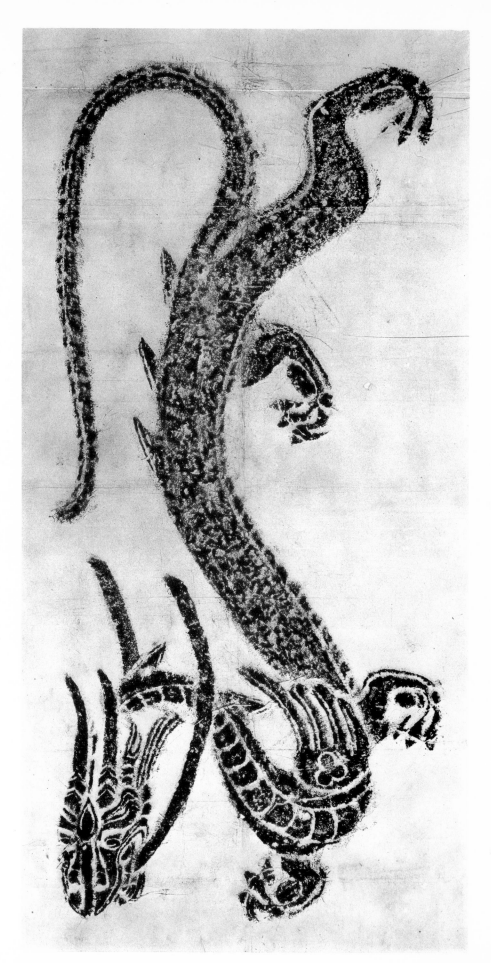

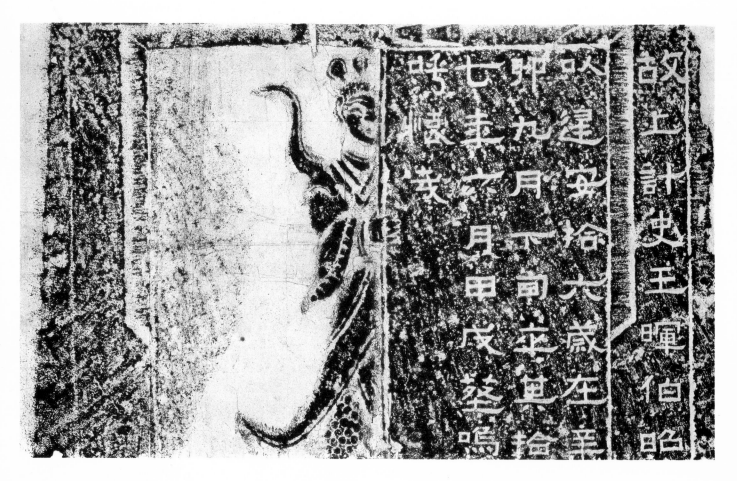

故上計史王暉伯昭

以運安拾六歲在
�平甘拾
七月下甲戌茇蓥鳴

75

RELIEFS ON BRICK AND TILE

SZECHWAN

77

78

80

81

83

84

85

86

87

88

89

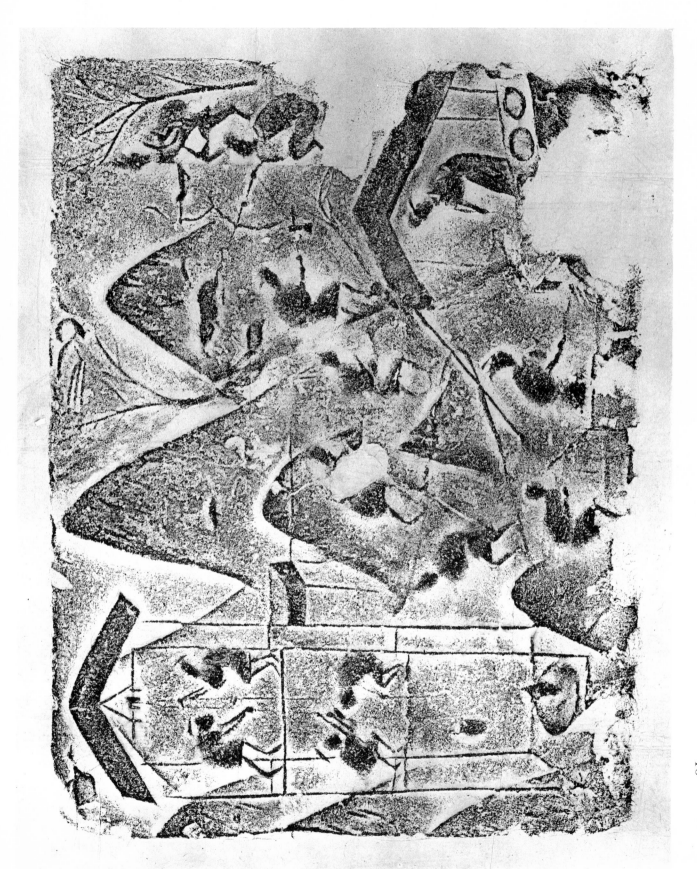

92

93

94

95

96

97

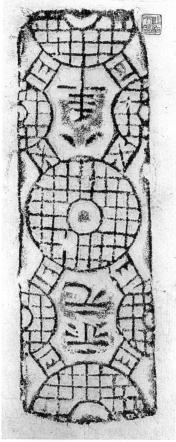

98

99